1

3

X

WHEN CORNISH SKIES ARE SMILING

When Cornish Skies Are Smiling

Denys Val Baker

WILLIAM KIMBER · LONDON

First published in 1984 by
WILLIAM KIMBER & CO. LIMITED
100 Jermyn Street, London, SW1Y 6EE

© Denys Val Baker, 1984

ISBN 0-7183-0525-6

Photoset in North Wales by
Derek Doyle & Associates, Mold, Clwyd
Printed in Great Britain by
Biddles Ltd, Guildford, Surrey

Contents

I

Down in the Valley

Living as we do in the heart of the winding Penberth valley just a few miles from Land's End – in an old mill house so secluded that it can only be reached down a narrow and very pot-holed lane – it is perhaps not surprising that our quota of 'normal services' is a very limited one. The lane, of course, is the problem: no matter how many expensive times we have strewn it with hard-core rubble, even once using a bulldozer to level things out, none of our improvements seems to survive for long – in no time, it seems, we are back to the customary era of bone-shaking drives in cars whose springs, even sometimes axles, are subject to regular breakages.

Faced with such a threat I suppose one must make allowances for some of our non-deliverers. British Road Services drivers, for instance, are naturally not only worried at what the pot-holes will do to their cumbersome and very large vehicles – they are also convinced, probably quite rightly, that because of its size the van will at some stage become permanently jammed between the narrow, grassy granite banks. (On the other hand the Aga fuel merchant regularly makes the perilous journey in his large tanker, cheerfully braving overhanging branches and other hazards – and just as well, too, as the warm heart of the mill house is entirely built around the cheerful red stove in our kitchen.)

The dustbin men – well it's true they have a large van, but we could wish they would show more enterprise, especially as we pay rather high rates for their services; alas, they remain impervious to our appeals, with the result that every Tuesday morning is a laborious occasion for me as I go round loading half a dozen heavy dustbins into the back of my Viva estate and then drive them up to the main road end of the lane, there to dutifully leave them awaiting the disdainful pick-up by the dustbin men (who therefore by my reckoning can hardly spend more than two hours a year working on our behalf!)

Unfortunately for us most other tradesmen making deliveries follow a similar custom – first timers who have never been before may brave the journey but usually only once, thereafter falling into the common habit – which is to leave all goods for us inside a small shed set up for that purpose at the top end of the lane. Even our milkman adheres to this system so that yet another of my onerous duties, a daily one this time, is to walk up and fetch half a dozen bottles of milk for ourselves and the other families scattered about the Tresidder estate.

Fortunately our other daily deliverer, the postman, is more considerate. Snugly ensconsed in his bright little red van he seems unworried about the undulating lane and daily drives all the way up to our front door, hooting cheerfully to let us know of his impending arrival. As a writer so very dependent upon communications I suppose I must count myself lucky in my relations with the post office – for instance when we lived at the Old Sawmills at Fowey, where there was no vehicular approach at all, every day the postman would walk nearly a mile along an old railway track in order to deliver our mail. So now here at Tresidder the tradition is nobly carried on, for which we are all duly grateful. Mind you, in the Fowey days – a time of hectic literary activity, including running the *Cornish Review* – the post seemed rather more important. Of late, largely because of inhibiting and persistent illness, I seem to write fewer letters and less and less articles, so consequently the postman's offerings are very much less in number. Unfortunately for me, with several of our children's families living around, the actual mail when it arrives seems large and only gradually, and disappointingly, do I realise that nearly all of it is for Mr S. Val Baker, or Miss Genevieve Val Baker or Mr Alan Moss, etc., etc.

Nevertheless, every now and then the postman brings me some special treat, and this happened one bright summer morning when he handed me a large rectangular package. I opened it curiously and revealed a delightful present in the form of a new book, *Poldark's Cornwall** by Winston Graham, inscribed inside in Winston's familiar spidery hand writing: 'For Denys and Jess: It's a bit like coals to Newcastle, but I thought you might like a copy. Very best wishes.'

Following this inscription Winston had printed an extract from one of his novels, *The Angry Tide*,† which indeed captured the whole flavour of what was to prove a remarkable book:

So they all went to look, at least as far as the stile leading down to the beach; further it was unsafe to go. Where the beach would have been at any time except the highest of tides was a battlefield of giant waves. The sea was washing away the lower sandhills and the roots of marram grass. As they stood there a wave came rushing up over the rough stony ground and licked at the foot of the stile, leaving a trail of froth to overflow and smear their boots. Surf in the ordinary sense progresses from deep water to shallow, losing height as it comes. Today waves were hitting the rocks below Wheal Leisure with such weight that they generated a new surf running at right angles to the flow of the sea, with geysers of water spouting high from the collisions. A new and irrational surf broke against the gentler rocks below the Long Field. Mountains of spume collected wherever the sea drew breath and then blew like bursting shells across the land. The sea was so high there was no horizon and the clouds so low that they sagged into the sea.

In his introduction to the book Winston explained that he had known Cornwall since he was sixteen and had lived there thirty years before moving first to France and then to Sussex, and that his association could therefore be divided into three phases. The first might be called the phase of delighted discovery; the second that of sun and sea addiction; and third that of nostalgic return. The first phase was experienced driving in his very first car, one of the early Morris Minors

* Bodley Head, 1983.
† Collins, 1977.

(later an equally rare Wolseley Hornet) – driving all over the county, up and down precipitous hills, round the endless blind corners, through narrow lanes with wind-crippled hawthorn trees crouching overhead and bramble and briar clutching as he passed, into and out of grey little villages, across the scarred moorlands with the sea shimmering in the distance ... and walked and walked the cliffs and the almost empty beaches which were as yet hardly aware of their future.

The second phase, says Winston, merged imperceptibly and overtook the first, essentially a pagan occupation of grilling one's body in the sun and then running down to the sea to enjoy body surfing – 'To come in on a wave on the north coast when a south-easterly wind is blowing, riffling the lips of the waves as they topple, is like being propelled landwards at great speed in a soda-siphon world.'

And finally the third phase was that period of great literary activity when, having written his first four Poldark novels in the 1940's and 50's, at last in the 1970's Winston found himself embarking on the ambitious sequels of *The Black Moon, The Four Swans, The Angry Tide* and *The Miller's Dance,* a somewhat strange experience:

From the consideration to the act was infinitely difficult. Whereas I have always moved easily, indeed with a sense of refreshment and challenge, from one style to the other, from the tauter, compact, modern novels to the more leisurely, broader-canvassed historical stories it was not so here; for I was not just reverting to another style, I was reverting to books already written long ago, picking up characters and situations, assuming and reconciling attitudes and differences, putting on clothes which – possibly – I had outgrown. I didn't dare to read the first four books through, for I knew if I did that that would finish it – only with sufficient dippings to refresh the memory. And I found to my surprise how much had been remembered; it was as if the characters had remained dormant in the subconscious, waiting for the word. Even so for the first hundred pages it was like breaking the sound barrier. Then everything began to move more steadily, more easily, as if predestined to a particular end.

Indulging myself hugely in enjoying Winston's autobiographical account I could not help being aware of another important aspect of *Poldark's Cornwall*, and one which I am sure Winston would wish me to praise – that is, the phenomenally impressive photographs by Simon McBride. There are more than 200 of these, almost all in dazzling colour, and I do not think in any other book have I ever seen the true heart of Cornwall so marvellously captured. The sepia view on the cover of the Cornish coast near Boscastle is indeed everyone's Cornish coast – vast and brooding, cruel and relentless, mysterious grey land enveloped by even more mysterious and ever restless sea. There are other marvellous views of the sea boiling at Treyarnon and caressing at Perranporth – and unusual watery aspects like the red river at Gwithian, the colour caused by the outflow from the copper mines.

Equally, of course, there are fascinating glimpses of the interior, lonely sights across Bodmin Moor, or aspects of old tin mines like Blue Hills and Botallack, or grey huddled village streets or perhaps some graceful town aspect like Walsingham Place, Truro – or the grandeur of famous family country homes like Trerice Manor near Padstow, or Lanhydrock near Bodmin. There is even a photograph or two of the tiny hamlet of Demelza, after which Winston named the heroine of his Poldark saga – a touch I appreciated for after mentioning seeing the name on a signpost and realising at once it was just right for the dark-haired waif whom Ross picks up at Redruth Fair, Winston goes on to explain:

> So Demelza became a girl's Christian name. The first girl to be so named in real life was Demelza Val Baker, the daughter of Denys Val Baker, the novelist and essayist. She must by now be well over thirty, but there have been many more since.

Yes, that was a morning to remember, the morning our friendly postman brought me Winston's offering ... and inevitably, I suppose, browsing through the wonders of *Poldark's*

Cornwall led me back, in a way, to consideration of our lane and our old house, our own little valley – to the nature of our little bit of Cornwall.

Well, to begin with, we do not immediately strike the Cornish note since we live in a valley, surrounded not by vast foaming seas, but by tall swaying trees. Ah, those trees – at once our blessing and our curse. For of course they are nearly all elms, and as such highly suspect; indeed more than one has collapsed on us, one recently just missing my office, another actually breaking its fall on a corner of Alan's studio, while perpetually the unfallen, the 'walking wounded', hang like everlasting threats – two leaning drunkenly over Demelza's caravan, and three poised menacingly above Genevieve's little chalet.

Even so, though officially terminal cases, our elm trees contain within their folds plenty of other signs of life – notably dozens of nests of rooks and crows chirping away as they greeted yet another season. We have grown so accustomed to the perpetual music of the rooks that we hardly notice the rather raucous noise, but visitors, of course, are at once struck – our equivalent, I suppose, to the sound of the sea lapping at the nearby shores. In addition to the rooks and crows we often play host to the visitors from further afield, such as red-crested woodpeckers, brightly plumaged kingfishers – and the occasional heron delicately stepping about the stream in search of often quite sizable trout.

Trees abound everywhere along the bottom level of our grounds but as the ground rises they fall away and at the very top stands our long field, bare of trees and occupied mainly by Jess's ambitious and ever growing vegetable garden, beans, peas, cabbages, beetroot, lettuce, spinach, tomatoes, potatoes – you name it, Jess is growing it. There are even a few grapevines left over from an originally ambitious planting of more than 100 – not enough, alas, to justify Château Tresidder of which we once dreamed. With a rotavator and many other gadgets, plus a huge plastic tunnel and two greenhouses Jess is very well equipped to produce much of our food – needless to say we spend many pleasant hours high up in her field, looking

out far and wide to Polgigga and Porthcurno and in the west to
Sennen, its tall church tower rearing up like a lighthouse.

Even so, not terribly Cornish in atmosphere – though the
name of our hamlet, Tresidder, is a good old Cornish one. I
had good reason to be sure of this for only recently out of the
blue had come an inquiring letter from one Frank Tresidder
who, though living up near Durham in the north of England,
obviously belonged originally to Cornwall – and was, as he
explained, engaged in researching the history of his surname.
And fascinating it all was, too. Apparently the original of
Tresidder as a name (and all its variations) might well go back
as far as 960 AD – however the earliest reference in document
form was in a paper dated 1297AD.

According to this the original name was 'Thresheder',
meaning 'village of the archers', of which there were three in
those days. It therefore followed that Tresidders did not have
one common ancestor but sprouted simulataneously from
three widely separated localities in Cornwall, without blood
ties. Books printed to date, Frank Tresidder told me, all
seemed to start with the name 'Wm de Treseder', in
Ecclesiastical Records for 1297, one even saying that the
original name was introduced by a man with French ancestry.

Frank Tresidder was obviously something of a live wire for
he had taken the trouble to write to every Tresidder he could
find in the Cornwall Telephone Directory. In this manner he
had charted more than thirty variations of the name, many of
which disappeared in the Middle Ages, probably through
epidemics. In Australia it had shifted in spelling from
Tresidder to Tressider – and Frank Tresidder could confirm
this in his own direct line to a common ancestry, born 1705 in
Wendron. Over the years, of course, the many Tresidders had
married into other families and the indefatigable Frank
Tresidder had traced some of these to Bolitho, Trethewy,
Tregowan, and Trewartha.

'By the way did you know that Tresidder Farm at St Buryan
was once one large estate but had been made into two adjacent
farms?'

Yes, we knew this, because in fact our own Mill House,

Tresidder, had also once been a single estate, later split into two. This matter was very much in our mind recently owing to the fact that against all the odds Alan and Gill's ambitious attempt (mentioned in *The Mill in the Valley*) had at last come to fruition, in that contracts had finally been exchanged for them to purchase Sheila Ley's adjoining property, Tresidder Mill – meaning in effect that once again the whole valley belonged to a single family.

From the beginning Gill and Alan obviously revelled in their new position of house-owners. They were constantly coming up and asking us to embark on yet another tour of their new property – and quite a tour it was, for Tresidder Mill was bigger than our place, the cascading stream wandering across two enormous flat fields with rising land up behind.

Totally different in character to the Mill House, the other property nevertheless had its own attractions. There were quaint little bridges and bowers and surprising little lawns, there was, too, the *Old* Mill House which Gill and Alan now proposed to rebuild and decorate and bring back to life. There were many other tasks to be done, of course, a new roof for the main bungalow, a new cesspit – and of course the perpetual problem of 'the lane'. This time we had decided to give it a covering of red shale which was supposed to be the best material for bedding down.

From the beginning Gill and Alan were anxious to involve the whole family – hence the first of a series of regular meetings at which we discussed all kinds of exciting possibilities – market gardening on Tresidder Mill's flat acres, mushroom growing in some of the old sheds, perhaps letting one or two caravans – cutting down some of the woods for firewood – keeping sheep, goats, ponies, chickens. Alas, the initial venture with our feathered friends went wrong – Jess went to an agricultural sale and came back excited with half a dozen chicks. She put them into a hut but unfortunately forgot about the perversity of Stephen's son, Paris who, could not resist the temptation of opening the door of the shed – with the result that all the chickens made a dash for what, not unreasonably,, they assumed would be freedom (but alas in due course would be meals for the local foxes).

Chickens were not Jess's only purchase towards developments on the new Tresidder estate. For a long time Stephen had been bemoaning the fact that many of our projects – like the planning of a garden patio outside our kitchen – were held up for lack of a serviceable tractor. Now, attending yet another sale, Jess managed to buy a second-hand tractor very reasonably, and the next day Stephen and Alan went over and drove it back in triumph. Now indeed things were moving in every sense of the word.

With the aid of our new 'toy', we were soon bumping around great granite rocks and changing the landscape. First we had knocked down the old pottery studio, always something of an eyesore – its functions having been taken over by Stephen's famous 'workshop', a huge building measuring 20ft by 20ft which had been nearly a year in the making but now, all at once, was miraculously finished. Within this spacious building were tool tables, work-benches and other surfaces, while down one wall ran the newly set up pottery kiln, wheels, glazes, etc. Here Gill and Genevieve hoped one day to get to work on producing decorated plates and tiles.

One way and other that autumn I am now remembering was indeed Keats' season of mellow fruitfulness, as one project after another was not merely announced – but set in motion. Alan and Stephen were the main workers, but Jess, Gill and Genevieve lent valuable help – I, alas, felt too ill to be of any practical assistance, but I gave what vocal encouragement I could, for I thoroughly approved of this total family venture. And indeed as I write now, it has gone from one achievement to another, with the result that gradually our new Tresidder empire is taking visible shape. That garden patio isn't finished, but it's coming on, with big paving slabs in place, plans for a swimming pool beyond and so forth. One way and another, in our own little valley, big changes are afoot.

II

Poetry in My Life

The persistent and nagging illness to which I have referred in one or two earlier books seemed to have become a permanent feature of my life – indeed only recently I had spent two weeks enduring another set of tests up at St Mark's Hospital, London. One effect is this constant 'downer' on my daily existence was an increasing difficulty in doing any work, certainly fiction seemed temporarily to have come to an end, and these days I was even having difficulty in pursuing my usually enjoyable autobiographical explorations.

One day, feeling the need for a change of mood I turned to one of the earlier loves of my writing life. Over the years I had always kept – secretly and not for publication – a steady supply of poetry, written in moods of happiness or depression, or of general meditation. I kept these in a file away from prying eyes: now, I thought I would take a look at what in effect amounted to nearly fifty years of Val Baker poems. Almost at once I came upon a timeless sort of poem, written many years ago and yet highly appropriate in what it now said:

Someone said how depressing it all was
And what a state the world was in
And would there be war with Russia
This year or next? And I agreed
Feeling the weight of too much suffering
Falling upon our shoulders like ghosts,
Sad residue of nineteen-fourteen
To nineteen-eighteen, of nineteen thirty-nine
To nineteen-forty five: and worse,

Of all the between years, barren and wasted,
Like a careless youth but without the innocence –
Feeling all this like a black and awful cloud
Blighting the present and the future
As much as the badly-expended past,
Leaving really very little hope.

And then I chanced to climb a sloping Cornish field
At the silent time of dusk, turning by the gate
And looking out upon a rich confusion
Of tiny fields, scattered farms, ungainly churches,
Still more ugly chapels, bleak skeletons
Of potters' chimneys, tinners' mines;
A white streak of the London train;
And on both generous horizons the sea
Lapping its avaricious boundaries.
Such a panorama, such an enormous vision
Of human geography – the space
That fell all around seemed more remote
Than the world's topical troubles;
And yet when the troubles are forgotten
The space remains, impregnable.

I watched an early star, rising with a yawn
Out of some other world's sleep. And all at once
The sour weights fell from my shoulders
And bounced, like hollow echoes, over the cliffs.
And I was left to see, clear as the dying sun
That silhouetted the rocky shadows of bygone days,
How very simple it all was
And not at all depressing
If you look at it the right way
And don't go chasing rainbows round the corner.

Have you ever lain upon a rock and watched the tide
Creeping over the day's trodden sands,
Leaving them virgin smooth for tomorrow?

Or watched a teacher's loving duster
Firmly erase the classes' arithmetic,
Leaving the blackboard bare for tomorrow?
Or sat in a speeding railway train
Whose journey obliterates each scene,
Leaving the canvas blank for the next view?

Well, then, is not life quite as simple a matter,
And certainly more enjoyable,
If we forget about the centuries
And the years and the months
And even the worrying weeks?
And simply remember:

Each new day
Is a new beginning
Is another existence.

Each new day
Is a new person
Is another world.

Each new day is contained in the palm of your hand,
In the twinkle of your eye, the sound of your voice
Saying Good-morning! – The first breath you draw
On waking. There was no yesterday,
Maybe no tomorrow, but there is each new day
To do with as you will. It is never too late
For anything except regrets. I am born
Each minute again – is that not the same way of saying
I die each minute – only a better way?
So why not begin to live again
Each new day?

Reading through these poems was a strange experience – in many ways like reviewing my life. There were many purely descriptive ones, like one I remembered being prompted to write after regularly travelling on the little red Grenville bus from St Hilary to Penzance:

Old women waiting to die in a bus
They are not really like the rest of us,
Happy or unhappy, glad of today,
Knowing that if it fails tomorrow may
Offer something new.

Look how they sit there like shrivelled grey birds,
Beaks rasping out harshly their fading words,
Feathers frayed, veins thick blooded, flesh skin-tight,
Old bones aching for the sleep of tonight.
They've nothing to do

Except look out of the window and see
Passing on their way to eternity
The fresh green fields, the golden gleaming land,
Familiarities they understand
Fading from their view ...

And so on. Then there were love poems, like this one:

My love came in the room
Bright as the morning rose
Alive as a flame
Soft as a song
Perfuming the air with her golden lust

My love came in the room
Sweet as the summer day
Her eyes were young
Her heart was full
Exciting the dead with her radiant life

My love came in the room
Warm with her secret promise
Of sun-kissed hands
And softly hands
Caressing the spot where the world begins

My love came in the room
Swift as any lover
We looked, we knew
Our love was true
And the marvelling jealous old world – stood still.

Often I found that I had been drawn to vivid images, just as I have
often been in prose. Thus I came across 'black sun in a white
sky, red daffodils on purple sea, magic motor cars driven
sideways, elephants pirouette with seagull wings, smoke from a
train frozen to stone.' And in another short poem I celebrated
our makers of myths who 'seize a virgin star out of the
motherless sky and with giant strides encompass land's infinity,
diving deep into green eyed waters ... '

Coming nearer to present times there was an interesting
poem I found about our round table in the kitchen at the Mill
House:

Our round table, our dear beloved round table
Sits in the middle of the familiar kitchen
Like a very old friend. Once hewn out of pine
And fashioned into life by a Cornish boy, David,
It has been our constant companion through so many years.
Can I really remember when it all began?
Oh yes I can, yes I can!

It was made for something quite different
From what it's become – a sturdy stand in a showroom
For hand-made pottery, displaying the goods
By which we precariously lived, along with writing,
The means of financing the relentless production
Of children – remember when it all began?
Oh yes I can, yes I can!

But later, swept clear of all goods and chattels
Our round table became what it was really intended
The centre of life, the focus of friends, the tip
Of the iceberg of love – the throne of family life

At which have gathered so many dear familiar faces
I lose count – remember when it all began?
Oh yes I can, yes I can!

How many meals, how many chairs, how many people
Have sat at our round table? A hundred, five hundred –
Perhaps a thousand, even more – what matters is the quality
For many in this world, not just our wandering family,
But all their friends and *their* friends – strangers, too –
Knew magic. Remember when it all began?
Oh yes I can, yes I can!

Times beyond counting we've sat enraptured around
Our beloved round table, plates piled high, glasses glinting
In mysterious candlelight – everywhere else in shadow
So that life and merriment can reign supreme
Between dear, dear loved ones and loved, loved dear ones
Together – remember when it all began?
Oh yes I can, yes I can!

Once four reflective souls sat around in peace
The next time fourteen gay laughters might be heard, no
    matter
The round table always had room for us all, that is its secret
And irreplaceable gift – like love it encompasses infinity
Providing a platform of floating nirvana in which we drown
All sorrows – remember when it all began?
Oh yes I can, yes I can!

Down the years our round table has groaned under weights
Of half a dozen people performing gymnastics
In drunken splendour – has been stained with wines red,
    white and pink
Drowned in candlegrease, been set fire to, faced every
    calamity
Yet survived them all: a coat of bleach, a sanding down, and
All was well – remember when it all began?
Oh yes I can, yes I can!

And then there was that special time, our Silver Wedding
When other minion tables were dragged in to extend the flow
Of gathered friends – but still our round table stood proudly
At the head of it all, and round it splendidly sat
Our eldest friends, toasting us in a sea of champagne. Ah those
Were the days – remember when it all began?
Oh yes I can, yes I can!

Since then the round table has been picked up and carried
Out into the sunshine, or into other rooms, or even on journeys
To some picnic place – yet it has always returned, like all our loves
To that same spot in the middle of the familiar kitchen
Like a very old friend who's been with us so many years
I can hardly remember when it all began – Ah, but yes, oh yes –
Yes I can, yes I can – Yes I can!

Poetry is, of course, a highly personal affair and many of my poems had been sparked off by personal dramas, difficult relationships with wife, children and so forth. In one I mused how one Saturday night found me all alone in a familiar and loved room with the yellow brown carpet and orange walls and the dark old dresser and the magical gold of our century old harp winking forever – 'And I thought of my love far away.' And strong memories came flooding back as I re-read a poem I once wrote when Jess was pursuing a life of her own. 'I wonder if a thousand miles away in that other world they call London you sometimes raise your head from books and stare out of some lofty window and watch the birds fly away, and have that sad feeling that makes you want to cry and cry and cry?'

In the same vein perhaps these lines will strike a chord with many a married couple, temporarily estranged:

Lying in bed with a stranger

Is this what our life's to become?
Beware, beware of the danger
The end of love's end has begun
Sitting at breakfast with someone
Already gone from the table
Come back, come back, oh that someone
While still, sweetheart, you are able.

Walking the streets towards somewhere
That no longer really exists
Because before we can get there
Love's lost in some unending mist

Coming home where home is the heart
Of such a golden universe
If only we could stop – then start! –
My dear, there'd be no need for verse.

Unfortunately more than other forms of writing, poetry does
seem to bring out the pessimism, like one of my last poems,
almost up to date in fact:

Will we remember the golden days
When we are dead?
Enjoy again those dear Cornish bays
When we are dead?
Sit on green clifftops in sunlit haze
When we are dead?
Surf again on those white-crested waves
When we are dead?
Watch sweet our children with loving gaze
When we are dead?
Embrace the world in a hundred ways
When we are dead?
Listen loving to what each other says
When we are dead?
Sit silent spellbound by sun's last rays
When we are dead?

Care any more where happiness lays
When we are dead?
Know if our love goes or if love stays
When we are dead?

Alas, alas, no more golden days
When we are dead.

Yes, I spent a fascinating period browsing through the poems
of my life, but by the time I had finished I realised that they
were, in effect, a complete entity: life experienced, and passed
by – no point in trying to resume the narrative, for somehow I
did not feel the same urge. All the same I did not feel
displeased to come upon such vivid evidence of memories of
the past.

III

Our Cornish Commune

The other day I heard that the Old Sawmills at Golant near
Fowey, for five years once our very beautiful and romantic
home, had been sold again. Strangely no one ever seems to
remain there for much more than the statutory five years or so
... And yet what a marvellous and unique place it is. Perhaps
stirred by this piece of news my mind drifted back in time –
and more especially to a very lively time soon after we moved
into the Old Sawmills.

As with so many activities in my life this one had quite a bit
to do with the blandishments of my daughter Demelza who,
with her friend Pacifist Pete, had done everything possible to
encourage the idea of buying the Sawmills.

Demelza and Pacifist Pete had a great many ideas, which as
yet I knew little about. They had decided for the moment to
play a waiting game, and to concentrate on getting Jess and me
well settled into our comfortable new home. Although not
exceptionally large, the house had a pleasant lounge with an
open fireplace where we could burn the logs which, at that
happy initial time, Stephen was vigorously cutting down with
axe and saw, and there was a nice airy kitchen and three
bedrooms. The largest of these we took for ourselves, another
was reserved for Genevieve on her holidays, and the third for
any odd guests.

Meantime Stephen, Demelza and Pacifist Pete had quietly
disposed themselves among the chalets, the sparse but
adequate furnishings of which we had taken over with our
purchase. The largest chalet, a little way up the valley, had been
chosen by Demelza and Pete. It was intended, though I did not

know this, as the nucleus or centre of the Cornish Commune.
By the time Demelza had hung up various weird psychedelic
posters and weavings, and portraits of John Lennon and Yoko
Ono and a few others, and Pacifist Pete had collected from the
local railway station several huge boxes containing his vast
library of philosophical books, the place looked quite a
home-from-home.

Stephen, on the other hand, had chosen the smallest of the
chalets, a curious two-roomed affair tucked into the side of the
hill a little way below our own house. Here he installed an old
Courtier Stove, and one or two other attractions, the most
notable being a complicated stereophonic tape system on which
blared tunes by Jimi Hendrix at all hours of the day and
night. He painted the walls of the tiny bedrooms orange and
black, and altogether made himself a cosy little cubbyhole,
which, he assured me cheerfully, he intended filling up from
time to time, at week-ends, with gatherings of 'the old gang' –
Stephen still suffered from the delusion that, because *he* had
walked out of university and turned his back on a formal
academic life, all his friends would have done the same. In fact,
such was the force of his personality when he chose to exert it,
and so strong the sentimental memories of the dear old days of
Stephen's youth, that there were several very jolly reunions in
that cosy little chalet.

In the meantime, we soon found ourselves encountering
problems with Stephen. Already Jess had found herself a
perfect patch of land for her ambitious garden, and was out
there every sunny morning digging and planting. Although I
still had to achieve my ambition of a writer's hut, I had
managed, temporarily, to rig up quite a pleasant working area
in the spare bedroom. For their part, Demelza and Pete
appeared to be busily engaged on projects whose nature
remained a mystery to me, but which involved periodical trips
into St Austell and other surrounding towns in my old Austin,
now kept in a farmer's barn at the nearest road point. At least
they were *occupied*.

Only Stephen, after a while, seemed at a loose end. At first
we thought of a method of solving this problem.

'Look here,' I said, 'until you've made up your mind just what you're going to do with your life' – oh, feeble, hopeful/hopeless words – 'supposing we make a straightforward business arrangement? For three months I'll employ you to do all sorts of odd jobs around the place – you can be a kind of estate manager, as it were. Goodness knows, there's enough work to be done. What do you think?'

At first Stephen greatly favoured the idea. It almost caused a temporary rift between him and the other two. Any kind of authority went straight to Stephen's head: in no time he was not only the estate manager, but behaving like one.

'Demelza and Pete, you'll just *have* to tidy up around your chalet. It's a disgrace to the estate.'

And again: 'Pete takes advantage of our fires. Why can't *he* cut some of the logs?'

This was a little unfair, as in fact Pete was always a willing and able helper, and often gave Stephen a hand with various enterprises. But I suppose Stephen had a point. It did seem to Jess and me that, although Demelza and Pete were living in one chalet, and indeed Stephen in another, most evenings seemed to end up with all of us sitting around the fire in *our* sitting-room, either talking or watching television. Worse, in a way, they began sharing our meals. At first it was just the evening one; somehow they would all be sitting round when Jess was preparing it, and so it seemed only natural and motherly to say: 'What about you lot, have you fed yet? Oh, well, have a bite with us.' Soon this was happening six nights a week – on the seventh, Stephen and Demelza and Pete went over to a folk club in Falmouth in *my* car – and after a while it tended to include lunch.

Only breakfast remained relatively sacrosanct. At breakfast time, Jess and I could creep down in to our own familiar kitchen, and brew a cup of coffee and make some toast, and sit staring out of the window watching for the familiar blue-coated figure of the postman. But then, of course, other eyes were also waiting for important letters. Within minutes of the post having arrived, they would be sidling in, Demelza and Pete, and then Stephen, to collect their mail … and that usually meant a cup of coffee all round.

Jess was very patient about it all, but naturally we began to get a little exasperated. She and I had not really arrived at this comparatively late stage of life expressly to play the roles of cooks and bottle-washers. There was a temporary alleviation when we worked out a complicated rota system, so that each person took a different night for cooking the main meals, but the general results of this were so disagreeable to the palate that I began to search around for some better solution.

'Look,' I said one day to Demelza and Pete, 'I've been wondering about you two. How are you managing?'

'Oh, that's all right, Dad. Pete has a bit of money saved. You don't have to worry.'

'Yes, yes. But I mean, when you came back from your travels abroad hadn't you some sort of – *plans*? Weren't you going to start something,' I said hopefully, 'on your own account?'

Demelza seized her unexpected opportunity.

'Oh, *yes*, Dad. We've *lots* of plans. Haven't we, Pete?'

'Sure.'

'The main idea is, you see, Dad, well, travelling around, I've been very struck about the need for young people to get together, talk over their ideas and so on. You know, international exchange and all that.'

'Yes, that sounds a good idea.'

My mind, as I nodded away, was really on other matters: the problem of Stephen's recurrent moroseness, a new idea for a book I was trying to work out, above all the problems of my writer's hut which loomed increasingly large in my mind. It would have been a far, far better thing if I had paid more attention to what Demelza was saying.

'Matter of fact, we've been getting in touch with quite a few people around – you know in Falmouth and so on – folk-singers, people like that, *free* people like ourselves. Well, it seems that what everyone really needs is some kind of a *centre*.'

'Yes,' said Pacifist Pete cheerfully. 'A co-'

Perhaps if he had uttered the fatal word it might have struck home somewhere, like a warning arrow from Fate or something. But Demelza interrupted hastily: 'So you see, Dad, the general idea is that perhaps we would start gathering together a few like-minded people. Up at our place of course.' The big chalet was already *her* place, just as the small one was resolutely *my* place to Stephen; it was just as well Jess and I had *our* house. 'It won't bother you at all, I can promise. We'll be *right* out of your way.'

Demelza gave me a brilliant smile, and took my arm in a delightfully daughterly way.

'What do you think? It's really putting into action some of those ideas I wrote you about in my letters.'

I looked at her with a father's natural affection. She really was, when all was said and done, quite a remarkable girl. Chip off the old block, I suppose.

'Yes, I enjoyed your letters,' I said, my mind somehow managing to blank out all those dreadful shocks and surprises and confessions and various other moments of incredulity and horror, as we read one startling sentence after another.

'Good,' said Demelza cheerfully. 'Then that's settled.'

For a while nothing untoward happened. Meantime we continued to be plagued by the continually irritating problem of Stephen. He had now decided that it was all wrong for him to be wasting his time doing odd jobs at his own home.

'I could live and die here and nobody would be any the wiser.'

'Surely that could apply to all of us?'

'Ah, yes, but *you're* old. I'm *young*. I'm supposed to be at the peak of my powers.'

Stephen frowned.

'What I want to do is to work with my body. I'm tired of using my mind.'

I could hardly see that he had been using his mind very much recently, mostly standing around chopping down inoffensive trees or attempting to erect dams for waterfalls. But I thought it wisest not to argue.

'What will you do then?'

Whatever we had imagined Stephen might do, his first choice quite outstripped any guesses. Somehow, through a friend, he heard of a job going as a night watchman on a dredger which was deepening the channel in the River Fowey not far away. By this time we had acquired a small but sturdy rowing dinghy which we used for making trips to carry groceries from the car and so forth, when the tide was right. It was proving, in fact, extremely handy, especially when we arrived back feeling rather tired at night and didn't fancy the ten minute walk along the old railway track. Stephen now appropriated this dinghy and rowed off in it towards dusk every evening, returning sometime after dawn, pale-faced and drawn-looking, to retire exhausted to bed for the whole day. It did not seem a very satisfactory arrangement. After a week, to general relief, he chucked it in – and we had the use of our dinghy again.

Stephen's next job was almost as brief, and equally bizarre. He became one of a gang of men who went around digging up sleepers from disused railway tracks for a contractor who later sold them at a fantastic profit. As defunct branch lines, though more common in Cornwall than many counties, were rather scarce, this meant that Stephen and the rest of the gang had to make a forty mile drive every morning to the site, and a forty-mile drive back at night, so that by and large he looked as tired and worn out as ever. Well, I supposed, he was certainly using his body.

Alas, after two weeks Stephen managed somehow to drop a two-hundred weight sleeper on his big toe and broke the bone. They took him to the nearest hospital and it was all bound up and put in plaster, and he was officially off work for six weeks, during which time, fortunately, he was able to draw sick pay.

But, of course, also during those six weeks, he was once again home. This latest Stephen, limping around in some pain and even more morose, drove us all nearly crazy.

'It's perfectly obvious what's the trouble,' said Demelza. 'Stephen needs someone to look after him.'

We all had to agree with this diagnosis, but the rest of us lacked the effrontery to do anything about the matter. Demelza had no such inhibitions. Besides, she saw at once a golden opportunity to further her more grandiose plans. Quite recently, Demelza had met, during one of her visits to the folk club at Falmouth, a girl who seemed to have made a big impression upon her. This girl had recently arrived back from a sojourn in Greece and was now very much at a loose end, in fact without anywhere to live. Remembering those prophetic words of the wise Provos: 'Someday *you* will be able to help someone else', Demelza had not hesitated.

'You must come and stay with us, of course. It couldn't be better – we're just starting our own commune.'

And so into our midst, and in particular into Stephen's midst, there came a small, determined, red-haired girl called Isolde. Whether that was her real name, or one adopted from ancient folktale, I never knew; but then somehow I am never sure that we ever knew Isolde, though at times we did try.

For one thing, initially, she was rather overwhelmingly commandeered by Demelza. It was a long time since I had seen Demelza so enthralled by someone, particularly another female. I think the clue to all this was that Isolde was a year or so ahead of Demelza in the pursuit of a rather similar career. Like Demelza, Isolde apparently had pathetically tolerant parents who had attempted sympathetically to go along with her various ideas – though I gathered that they were considerably wealthier, with a large house and a swimming pool and other appendages. Like Demelza, but more widely, Isolde had travelled the international highways and byways – not merely Holland and France, but Sweden and Denmark, Germany and Italy, even as far away as Morocco.

Finally, she had spent an apparently rather uncomfortable winter living with a group of meditative hippies in some rather barren caves on a lonely Greek island. There, presumably, had existed something of the same general philosophical atmosphere, though obviously not the comfort, that Demelza had encountered at the Château de Fontenoy. People coming together in communion, shedding all their greed and possessiveness, joined by love – the beautiful people.

'They often only had goat's milk to drink and a few dates and berries,' said Demelza, wide-eyed. 'They were vegetarian, so they couldn't eat the fish. But they survived somehow.

Everything was communal. They used to clip the goat's hair to make up clothes ... '

Goats appeared to have made a lasting impression upon Isolde, who, we were to discover, not only loved all people but all other living creatures as well. After a brief reunion with her parents she was off on the open road again, attired romantically enough in some coloured shawls which she had brought back from Greece. Isolde was an independent young thing and had painfully acquired the ability to crochet her own shawls with the idea of earning a precarious living in this fashion. At the time Demelza met her, she was renting a caravan in a field above the Lerryn river – that is, as I was about to say, Isolde plus her two recently acquired Cornish goats, Elbow and Ankle.

When Isolde first appeared at the Old Sawmills, it was without the goats and all I had was a brief glimpse of quite a pretty little redhead, somehow slightly depressing in her voluminous cloaks and shawls on a hot spring day, and looking rather earnest, too. In no time Demelza had whisked her off to show her around Stephen's chalet, hers and Pete's chalet, the other outbuildings, the stream, the orchard, the fields. I did not realize it, but Isolde, for her part, was casing the joint on behalf of the goats ...

When Isolde finally moved in, Jess and I happened to be sitting at the kitchen window, looking out over the placid scene. The tide was up, the whole creek glimmered and glistened, and tall trees were reflected in rippling rows. In the distance the old railway line forked across the end of our property, our only link with civilization. Suddenly, along this link, the procession appeared. First, Demelza, proudly leading the way, herself wearing an extraordinary Moroccan outfit, hooded cap and all, which Isolde had given her, so that she looked like a monk. Next, the honoured guest herself, red hair flaming in the afternoon sun, and a firm square set of the shoulders that boded lots of grim determination for the task in hand. Then, somewhat surprisingly, Stephen, almost loaded to the ground with parcels, cases and a huge gourd.

'Aha!' said Jess, knowingly.

And then, rather like items emerging one by one from the Ark, they came: first one goat, then a second goat, then a pig, then a dog, then a cat; and finally, carried in a square cardboard box by a rather worried-looking Pacifist Pete, whose other duty had obviously been to keep the pig and dog and cat from straying, there was the last but not the least: Harriet, the pregnant hamster.

'Do you see what I see?'

'I do, indeed.'

'They're coming here!'

'Undoubtedly.'

'But I mean – I never said – Demelza didn't – '

Relentlessly the advancing column advanced; up along the woodland path, down through the green slopes to our quayside, and along the side of our house, but fortunately onwards and past it. Jess and I watched, breathless, our ears catching for the first – but not the last – time these new and unfamiliar community sounds: the petulant brayings of Elbow and Ankle, the grunts of Greta the pig, the growls of Hywel the Welsh collie, the occasional uncertain miaows of a Siamese cat whose name I never caught, but who was also, it later transpired, pregnant; and finally, fleetingly, a sound with which later I was to become pathetically familiar: the sudden terrified bleating of Harriet the hamster, as she sensed some unseen danger approaching – or imagined she did, which had just the same effect on her vocal chords. After what seemed an exceedingly long time, the entire straggling column vanished higher up into the estate, to be deployed hither and thither, though not, as we were quickly to learn, with any sort of permanency.

I have described Isolde's arrival at some length because it is important to make clear how overwhelmingly, for a while, this event occupied our minds. Under the impact of such an alarming invasion I naturally paid little attention to anything else. After all, how could I? Within less than an hour I was helping Pete and Stephen in desperate attempts to recapture Greta the pig, who didn't appear to like her new environment and made a desperate run in the general direction of Fowey.

Later the same day I had the ignominy of being chased half-way up a tree by a malignant black-faced goat which I came to recognize, in time, as Elbow – though Ankle, I discovered, was quite liable to treat me in the same fashion. None of the animals, it appeared, wished to stay put anywhere, and were always wandering off. If ever there was a moment of quiet, then Hywel would suddenly have a fit of mad barking, rushing round and round, and in response the Siamese cat would set up an unholy kind of wailing. Inevitably, the effect of all this would be to distract still further the perpetually distracted Harriet, and her extraordinary bleep-bleep messages would shriek all over the creek.

Some of these things happened at once, others during the next few days. The result, as I say, was that our whole attention had to be applied entirely in the direction of these new threats. Consequently I hardly noticed the gentle infiltration of other objects, besides goats, a pig and various domestic animals. Not many at first: just one or two, maybe three or four. Possibly they sidled across the railway line at night, perhaps they even swam up river like homing salmon – I don't know, I only know that, gradually, in my travels, I became aware of a few extra bodies accumulating about the place. Not exactly the sort of bodies one could miss either: a tall bony young man with fuzzy hair and beard down to his navel; a gypsy-type girl without a gypsy's vitality, somehow bowed down as by invisible cares – in this instance, it transpired, infant cares. There was something about them depressingly enervating; they almost visibly communicated a painful sense of weariness to me. Yet these were, did I but know it, the beginnings of the Cornish Commune.

'I think you should have a word with Demelza,' said Jess one day. 'When I was working on my patch today I saw at least half a dozen completely strange people eating a meal outside their chalet. They're obviously *living* there.'

'Don't worry. I'll find out *just* what's going on.'

Somehow, like all such conversations, my talk with Demelza seemed to get bogged down somewhere. She reminded me how unanimously we had agreed earlier on the need for young people getting together and exchanging ideas and so forth: that was really all that was happening, she assured me. Just a few like-minded folk living up in the woods. There was absolutely no need for me to worry – it wouldn't interfere in any way with my life. She would *personally* see to that. Although, of course, if there was ever any job I wanted done, however menial, I had only to ask and help would be forthcoming at once ...

In the meantime, what did we think about Isolde and Stephen?

Alarmed, my attention immediately diverted, I waited to hear about Isolde and my only son. It was true that recently we had noticed Stephen displaying a curious tendency to follow Isolde about, just like the goats and the pig and the dog and other animals. Something was obviously brewing.

'Super, isn't it?' said Demelza.

'What's super?'

'Oh, didn't you know? They're getting together.'

'You mean they've fallen in love?'

Demelza shrugged.

'I wouldn't say that. Isolde is an awfully kind person. She's always trying to help people. I've been telling her about Stephen's problems. She quite understands. She's moving in to the chalet.'

In these free and easy days, it was hardly for us to express any real objection to whatever domestic arrangements Stephen chose to make; he was, after all, an adult now, one supposed. The fact this proposition seemed to us almost certainly doomed to disaster, was hardly the point.

Besides, any initial anxiety we might have felt for our son's well-being was quickly swept away by very real problems which the new move brought to us, ourselves. For when Isolde moved, her entourage moved too. It must be admitted that she made creditable efforts to keep her goats and the pig tethered away up in the orchard. It made no difference. Once they had sensed that their mistress had removed herself to Stephen's chalet, to Stephen's chalet they came, dragging their ropes and broken stakes resolutely behind them. And since, unfortunately, Stephen's chalet was only about fifty yards from our own house, we became perpetually involved as well. Frequently we would come into the kitchen to find Elbow and Ankle standing in a corner eating from our vegetable rack. On other occasions Hywel would wander in and urinate on our fireplace – some Freudian kink he developed which could never be eradicated. Greta the pig once charged right through the house, in the front door and out the back door, leaving a trail of havoc, but we usually kept a wary eye out for her and blocked most attempts, and anyway she preferred waddling up to the patch and eating Jess's lettuces and carrots and spring onions. Harriet the hamster was at least confined to a box and a wire run, but it was placed alongside the main path, and I was constantly being caused a minor heart attack as Harriet would suddenly bleep-bleep at the distant sound of my approach.

One day, fearing that I might have a nervous breakdown over all these matters, Jess said, very sensible: 'Why don't you stop bothering and get on with building that writer's hut you're always talking about?'

It was, the more I thought about it, a very sensible idea. A real therapeutic brainwave. There and then I went in diligent search of the axe and saw, which Stephen invariably dropped wherever he had last been using them, and set off up into the woods. I had already previously earmarked a possible site, although apparently that must have been on a particularly sunny day, for now it all seemed rather gloomy. Still, not to worry, there was nothing that man's ingenuity could not solve if properly directed. Busily I set to with axe and saw, felling innocent trees all round me in a single operation with a double purpose, first to clear a space for the hut, secondly to provide the wood with which to build it. Simple really.

I spent a whole week erecting my hut. It proved, of course, to be a far from simple operation, and in any case the finished object would no doubt have been rejected by any building expert. However, the fact was, that as day followed day, a building began to take shape: not exactly symmetrical by any means, extremely rough-looking, but, well a kind of writer's hut. I was, it is true, increasingly worried about the lack of light. It was beginning to seem that, though I had left spaces for two windows, I was going to need some form of artificial lighting simply in order to see to write. However, with the arrival of the week-end, I decided to leave matters for a couple of days. As a matter of fact, Jess and I had the brilliant idea of slipping off for a weekend down at St Ives with some of our old friends. We returned, very much refreshed, on the Monday morning.

'Well,' I said to Jess, after we had a cup of coffee and glanced through the post. 'I think I'll be going along to my hut.'

'Shall I come too?'

'Yes, do. That'll be nice.'

It was as well I took Jess with me, otherwise I might have committed some kind of violent act. When we reached the small glade in which my hut had been ingloriously erected, we found the trees festooned with small articles of clothing being dried. Outside the hut, a small, very dirty, naked child was playing. Inside, when dramatically I flung open the heavy door, built of sliced tree trunks, there were two young people lying comfortably in sleeping bags on the floor.

They sat up and looked up at us calmly and innocently. The man was sensitive-looking, with a faint straggling beard and pleasant cool grey eyes; the girl, if I had been in a mood to recognize it, was rather pretty in an elfin fashion.

'Well, hullo there, then,' said the young man in the friendliest manner. 'Greetings, friends. I'm Arthur, and this is Sue. Who are you, then?'

I struggled unsuccessfully, to find words. Jess took over.

'We were just wondering – you see, my husband has only just *built* this hut –'

The young man looked politely interested.

'Is that so, man? Well, I guess we're very grateful. Any roof over one's head is – well, you know how it is.'

I found my voice at last.

'You were *told* to come here?'

'Oh, of course. We were ever so grateful, weren't we, Sue?'

'Oh yes, ever so grateful.'

The elfin girl fluttered her eyelids in ecstasy.

'It's right out of this world, it really is. Back to nature.'

'Demelza?' I said grimly.

The young man looked a little bewildered.

'Why yes, that's right. She said there were *lots* of old buildings around, huts and things, and we were just to take our pick. That is for the time being. Until they get up some of the wigwams.'

'*Wigwams?*'

Jess pressed my arm gently.

'Dear, I think perhaps – '

I stood looking around the hut. Funnily enough, I found my anger subsiding. I could see suddenly that it was totally unsuited for a writer's hut: too dark, too cramped, too ... Hell it was just a botched-up job!

'Oh, never mind,' I said impatiently to the puzzled young man and his girl-friend, to Jess, to the air. 'You can stay here. I don't want it!'

I turned and began striding along the path. Jess began hurrying to keep pace with me, eyeing me anxiously.

'Do stop running! I thought you said you *did* want a writing hut.'

'Oh yes, indeed.' I nodded my head vigorously, but went striding on. Already the idea was formulating in my mind. At last we came out of the wood and down to the lawn below the house.

'There,' I said with a flourish, pointing to the small quay on the opposite side of the creek. '*That's* where I'll build my hut. Plenty of light, and completely cut off from all distraction. But this time I won't try and build it myself. Oh no! No, I'll buy one of those ready-made worksheds. You know, you see them advertised in the week-end magazines. Just the job.'

IV

A Visit from the Film Makers

When it finally arrived, my twelve by ten foot cedarwood shed proved indeed eminently satisfactory, once we had overcome a few initial difficulties – like having to tow it in the water down river to get it to the house, and then tinker about somewhat with the windows, none of which seemed able to keep out draughts. And then, of course, there was the slight oversight on my part about the occasional high tides. I just forgot all about this particular problem, with the result that one day in May I was sitting proudly in my new writer's hut typing away at some epic when I became uncomfortably conscious that my feet were cold and rather wet. Looking down, I saw to my horror that not only my feet but the whole floor of my new working home was completely encompassed by a malevolent, implacable rising tide of water. Jumping up and peering out of the window, I could see nothing but water everywhere, surrounding me in all directions. Panicking, I threw open the window and yelled out all over the creek.

'Help! I'm sinking! Someone come and rescue me, for God's sake!'

I was faintly astounded to discover that my panic-stricken calls brought forth a bevy of able-bodied men from all directions, several of whom dived into the water and started swimming to my rescue. However, I thought the most sensible behaviour really was that of a big black-bearded man who calmly got into our dinghy, unshipped the oars, and rowed over until he was directly under my window. I stepped into the boat quite easily, and the bearded man rowed me quietly back to the other side.

'Well,' I said, stepping thankfully on to dry land. 'I must say that was very helpful of you. I don't think we've met, have we? I suppose you're one of Demelza's friends?'

The bearded man smiled, in a quiet, rather soothing way.

'That's right. My real name's Harry.' He smiled again. 'But most of my friends call me Jesus.'

Then with another friendly nod he loped off towards the woods.

Meanwhile, all around, I became aware of other would-be rescuers still thrashing about in the water. Feeling awkward, I waved my acknowledgement.

'Thanks! Thanks very much for trying to help.'

At first I felt a worried sense of responsibility for causing them to get their clothes wet, until after a while it dawned on me that they were actually rather enjoying themselves, swimming around in the wide creek. It was a lovely sunny afternoon, the tide was high – indeed what better way to spend the time?

I went up to the house and called out to Jess.

'Hey – what about coming for a swim?'

Soon we were having our first dip of the year in our own creek, and it was rather marvellous. After a while, Demelza and Pete came and joined us, and later Isolde and Stephen. I could still not get used to the idea, but there it was.

Isolde had moved firmly into the small chalet, everything was neat and tidy and efficient – or at least, as efficient as could be in an establishment into which goats and pigs wandered at will, and where only the day before the Siamese cat had delivered herself of six sturdy infants. Stephen appeared to be fed regularly and no longer plagued our larder. What other favours he received was none of our business. We assumed there must be some kind of relationship, but all the same they seemed to me a curiously disjointed pair. Nothing they did together ever really seemed harmonious. It was so now: once in the water, Stephen raced about like a gay amphibious animal, but after a short dip Isolde was out again, fussing about her damned goats. I looked at Jess and raised my eyebrows but said nothing.

After that debâcle we had to raise the entire hut on to stilts made out of concrete blocks, and then finally it was safe from the occasional rogue tide and I was free to get on with my work again. It would hardly be true to say that work received my undivided attention. One of the interesting aspects of my new position was that it provided a grand-stand view of practically everything going on at the Old Sawmills. I was omnipotent. I could see Stephen's chalet, the goats, the pig, the dog, the cat, the hamster, our own house. Jess's patch ... and more, much more. I could see right up the valley to the big chalet, to the other sheds, to all the various signs of workers toiling on the common land.

By now, Demelza had gently broken to me, in rather more detail, the general idea of the Cornish Commune. It was true that often there seemed very little similarity between the idealistic and perfected organization which she described in such lyrical terms and what I saw with my own critical eyes. At that early stage, her commune looked like a run-down refugee camp. Nevertheless, I told myself grimly that, in these times of ultra-materialism, it was an admirable thing for the young to have ideals. Why should not these ennobled souls at least have the chance to return to Mother Earth, grow their own foods, live their own lives, follow their own Karmas?

The way Demelza put it, I had to admit it sounded quite attractive. She spoke one day almost uninterruptedly for nearly an hour about the whole project, which I thought an impressive if rather exhausting feat. There were, nevertheless, quite a few points I intended to take up firmly: questions and rather important objections to one or two proposals. Unfortunately, just at that moment, out of the kitchen window, horrified, I spied Elbow and Ankle nudging open the door of my new shed, and their ungainly bodies disappeared inside. With a cry of despair, I left Demelza standing and ran like hell to reach the hut before my precious manuscripts were nibbled away.

So it seemed as if I never altogether got a chance to pin Demelza down about my objections. She had repeated most earnestly her assurance that the commune would keep to its own 'scene' higher up the valley, and would not dream of intruding upon my own privacy. For the rest – well, at least from my new vantage point I was able to keep a close eye on events, the comings and goings, trying to suppress a curious conviction that there always seemed more of the former than the latter.

I did not always too much like the look of some of the various fuzzy-haired hippies and beats, but when I said so, Demelza attacked me for my racial prejudice and prevailed on me to attempt to widen my education in the matter. In this way, somewhat to my surprise, I encountered a succession of quite likeable and genuine eccentrics who appeared devoutly bent on such bizarre pursuits as composing music for the harpsichord, carving weird statues out of old clumps of my beech trees, fashioning lumpy bowls and mugs out of clay dug up from the ground, or merely standing on their heads for an hour or so each day, meditating.

Then, in addition to the resident members of the commune, there were a lot of daytime visitors to Isolde, local devotees she had somehow accumulated.

'She's so kind, you see,' explained Demelza. 'She's always rushing around trying to help people, you've no idea. Poor Isolde, she's always giving herself so much – she'll wear herself out.'

It did not seem to me that Isolde was exactly wearing herself out on Stephen's behalf, but is was certainly true that she seemed to attract disciples. The majority of them seemed to be men: young bearded men and old bearded men and bald priest-like men from Eastern countries; where they all came from I never quite knew, but quite often five or six would be assembled in Stephen's chalet, sitting around in a circle worshipping at the shrine of Isolde.

Often, we gathered, there was really no room for Stephen at all, and he took to coming over to the house and sitting morosely watching television in the sitting-room. We did not like to say anything. At the end of Late Night Line Up Stephen would stand up, sigh wearily, and say: 'Well, good-night,' and return – to what kind of reception we could not possibly imagine.

Meantime, the fact that there was considerable local gossip and speculation about activities at the Old Sawmills only dawned on Jess and me gradually. In our naivety and innocence, it had not really occurred to us that middle-aged *we* could in any way be confused with the younger generation. We assumed that, just as we allowed them to get on with their lives, so would other people.

We, for our part, felt it incumbent upon us to be ready to make overtures to our new neighbours: indeed, we could have done with some friends of our own age group. So periodically we made our efforts. We called in at the nearest pub, a pleasant building down on the main river; investigated the possibility of joining the local sailing club; and of course, benignly attempted to join in the general chatter at the local grocery shop and the local sub post office. In all these establishments our reception was the same; there was a coolness, or, to put it more bluntly, a decided hostility.

'It's a pity,' I said to Jess. 'I mean, I had somehow imagined becoming at least a part of the local community.'

Just once, almost like a miracle it seemed at first, we were invited to a local bigwig's house for cocktails. Of course, I realize now that he must have been agog with curiosity to see what sort of species we were. However, there was really very little opportunity for many pleasantries. We had hardly had time to enter the luxurious house and thankfully grasp our first cocktail before we became aware that everyone in the room was crowding round the bay window, staring at some passing spectacle.

Uneasily, Jess and I gathered on the fringe. Outside we spied a series of only too familiar figures slinking steadily down the road, on their way home from some outing: Isolde and some of her followers, a couple of flower girls, some bearded hippies, and bringing up the rear the big man called Jesus.

All conversation in the sitting-room was at a standstill, all glasses were held poised indefinitely in mid air, and everyone, including ourselves, watched in fascination until the esoteric group had finally disappeared.

Then the babble of cultured, middle-class voices broke out.

'What – ?'

'Who – ?'

'Why – ?'

'Tell me,' said an aristocratic-looking lady with very much raised eyebrows, 'what on earth are those – those *creatures* doing in our village?'

Cravenly, Jess and I said nothing, as if there could not possibly be any connection between neatly dressed conventional us and those – those creatures. But, of course, most of the people in the room must have known there was only one destination that lay along the distant railway track.

'Mmmmh, yes.' Our host, a bluff, jovial, red-faced retired officer, coughing and spluttering with a certain amount of embarrassment, obviously felt it his duty as an officer, to speak his mind.

'Don't know what the country's coming to, really. Up to no good, I'll warrant. Modern youth!'

He raised his bushy eyebrows almost as high as the aristocratic lady's, and then, remembering the gentlemanly part of his duties, gallantly offered Jess and myself another drink. We refused politely and as soon as was decently possible slipped away.

When we walked back along the railway track, we were strangely quiet.

I continued to grow very angry with Demelza about the Cornish Commune, of course. Despite all the blithe assurances, it seemed to me that there were all kinds of valid complaints, and almost every day I would find myself marching resolutely along the tangled woodpath towards the distant encampment. As I did so, I would hear ahead of me the variety of sounds: strumming guitars, baritone voices, wailing flutes, thumping axes, spades clinking on stony ground, now and then the reverberating, hideous whine of a small power-saw at work. This was the period of the creation of the famous 'wigwams', the idea of a strange, wraith-like figure called Bruce, who lived the wigwam life during a sojourn out in California. Somehow he had actually built four wigwams and set them in a semicircle around the main chalet. Their ingredients seemed to me mainly branches and bracken and mud, and I could not help wondering what might happen when it rained, but Bruce assured me with touching enthusiasm that everything would remain intact.

That was the trouble. Every time I went up, bent on having a row, I ended up becoming fascinated by some new aspect of what was going on. The wigwams, the crocheting, the wood-carving, the clay-modelling, the scheme for growing tobacco: they all seized on the imagination. Besides, there were some real signs of what might be called economic viability. Crops were being planted, some hens had been obtained – how, exactly, I thought it best not to inquire – and there were plans for baby piglets, more goats, even some cows, and schemes were afoot for selling things to local householders, rather in the style of the gypsies.

'You see, Dad', said Demelza enthusiastically, 'we don't need much money – we just share our possessions anyway. Everything becomes different when you look at it like that. Oh, I do wish I could explain to you. It's a marvellous kind of freedom. We're *independent*.'

Even though I felt this was not a strictly accurate statement – I myself had occasionally put a few pounds into the kitty, as I felt pretty sure had the parents of Isolde, and maybe of some of the others; though to be fair, when really necessary, some of the stronger lads periodically went off to earn money picking cauliflowers and potatoes for local farmers – even so, I found myself increasingly impressed by what Demelza said and, as time went by, what I saw happening. In a world such as we grown-ups had created, there seemed something curiously – well, *pure* about what was going on here in the valley.

I used to return to Jess shaking my head helplessly.

'I suppose by rights we ought to turf them out.'

'Well, you might then at least get on with some of your own work.'

'Yes, of course, darling. I do agree. All the same ...'

I would shake my head again, puzzled. At last I would heave a sigh, mostly of relief.

'Ah, well, the great thing is really that it's not our worry, is it? I mean, it's Demelza's responsibility. We're just spectators.'

Eventually, as we had anticipated, Stephen passed through the whole gamut of his Isolde phase and emerged, puzzled, at the other end of the scale. I could sympathize with him: apparently, at one stage, the six kittens lived in the chalet as well. In the long run, he simply got fed up with Isolde's perpetual retinue, and her incredible involvement with so many lame ducks, rushing hither and thither. When it reached the stage where he was not even getting his meals, that for Stephen represented a breaking point, and there was a big and final row. I was glad however, that he showed some magnaminity, even though for a moment the prospect of an Isoldeless Old Sawmills offered rosy visions.

'Oh, we can't actually ask her to go, Dad,' Stephen shook his head, bewildered, just as the rest of us did when we contemplated the facts. 'I mean, how could we? She's got *so many things with her.*'

So Isolde was left in sole possession of Stephen's chalet, and Stephen moved into our spare room ... and for a while the three of us withdrew into what you might call an internal commune of our own. Just briefly, I think we all found it rather pleasant. While further up the valley mammoth decisions were being made, projects starting and foundering, rows blowing up, wild accusations being thrown around, indeed all the hallmarks of communal life in the raw, we three went quietly about our business. Stephen acquired yet another of those bizarre occupations to which he seemed drawn, entering into partnership with a roguish young man from Polruan who owned an old lorry. The two of them went round collecting scrap and when they had a full load they drove all the way up to Exeter, where they had discovered they could get a very much higher price than locally. I think that, while up there, Stephen possibly renewed contact with an old London taxi salesman friend, because there were hints of scrap operations abroad in the near future.

Meantime, most evenings, Stephen would eat with us and afterwards we sat cosily by the fire watching television and relaxing pleasantly.

'Of course,' I said prophetically to Jess one night. 'This can't last.'

The very next day, looking out of my workroom window, I saw what seemed a veritable expedition straggling along the railway line. There were several human beings, but stranger objects as well: what looked like machines, large black boxes, elongated pieces of metal, scientific antennae ...

'Cameras, I fancy.' Jess, who happened to be with me at the time, looked out with interest. 'Cameras and tripods and recording equipment, and miles and miles of electrical cable ... '

Incredibly, she was right. Half an hour later, almost delirious with excitement, Demelza was introducing me to a square, round-faced, bald-headed American called Walter, who, she announced proudly, had brought his film unit all the way to the Old Sawmills especially to take a film of the Cornish Commune.

'But – how on earth did he hear about it?'

'Oh,' Demelza looked a little evasive. 'These things get around you know. I've told quite a few people. You must appreciate, Dad, this is something quite new.'

'Yeah,' said Walter, who actually, as in the caricatures I had seen of film directors, carried a perpetual stub of a cigar, which he shifted from side to side of his mouth when he spoke. 'You can say that again, baby. Jesus, just finding the darn place! And then the goddam walk.' He wiped the perspiration from his broad brow, and then looked around him, more cheerfully.

'Jesus, but if this ain't the big one! Whadya think, Hal?'

'Great,' said Hal, the chief cameraman, who was as tall as his employer was short. 'Just great.'

'Well, whadya think, boys?' repeated Walter, looking round at his entourage. At first sight it had seemed enormous, but I was relieved now to see the total of actual human beings was only five.

'Sure, Walt,' they chorused. 'It's a wow.'

'Tell you what, Walt,' said Hal learnedly, after darting about a little, and climbing a tree to take a quick view, and so on. 'We'll use plenty of zoom lenses ... Oh, great panning! Can't you just see? That water – that light – those trees!'

Walter looked dubious.

'Yeah, what about the *light*, Hal? We're going to have a problem there.'

'Problem, Walt?' Hal gave a laconic grin. 'Problems are our business.'

What their business actually was, Demelza explained to me in a voice still trembling with excitement, was to travel all round the world filming what was *really* going on in the Underground Movement.

'Underground Movement? I thought it was my retirement home?'

'Oh, Dad. You know what I mean – up in our part.'

'Ah, yes, of course. Your part.'

'The Cornish Commune is something unique. That's why Walter's come all this way to film it. It's a great honour – why, usually he's filming in Amsterdam and Paris and London, doing living theatres, group therapy gatherings, that sort of thing; but when he heard about us, well, he said he felt he just had to come and get us on film.'

I tried to grapple with a few relevant points. Just who exactly would see these films of Walter's?

'Why, people in the Underground Movement, of course.'

'But I mean, isn't it all a bit costly – filming and so on?'

'Oh, yes.' Demelza looked suitably impressed. 'It's *very* costly. But it doesn't matter, because Walter's got help from all kinds of places.

'Are you sure they quite understand what Walter's doing?'

'Oh, of course,' said Demelza impatiently. She wasn't really interested in such mundane details.

'Do you know, as soon as they've done this film they're going straight off to *India*! They're going to film all the great mystics out there, visit their retreats and all that. Won't it be *fabulous*?'

'Yes, stupendous. By the way, how on earth do they get around with all that stuff?'

'Haven't you seen? They've got a huge sort of Land Rover thing. It's parked back in the village. Walter says it holds two thousand pounds worth of equipment. It's got bunks and a cooker, too. They can travel in it all over the world.'

Demelza was perfectly right. I took a walk down the railway line later and saw Walter's vehicle. It was difficult to miss it as it had been left blocking a large part of the road into the nearby village, and appeared to be causing considerable annoyance among the local residents. I made appeasing sounds and appeals to their snob complexes.

'So sorry, but you know – *film* people.'

I had a good look at the van, which was certainly enormous. It had extra large tyres and an elongated body with a raised roof. It was really like a travelling pantechnicon. Some member of the unit, obviously proud of the travel quota, had stuck labels along one side of the vehicle: Big Sur – San Francisco – New York – Paris – Amsterdam – Copenhagen – London. I looked thoughtfully at the blank spaces left. Soon no doubt there would be a new label: Cornwall. And then, after that, the unpronounceable name of some remote Indian mystic's retreat.

I shook my head, oppressed by a curious sense of unease, and walked back along the railway track. I felt I would be glad when the film company and their disruptive presence had gone.

They were certainly not staying long. Demelza told me when I got back that the whole unit had to be at Southampton the next afternoon to catch the boat to India. So they planned to get on with their filming all day while the light lasted, then they would use some spots and things. I wouldn't mind if they connected up a few cables, would I?

'I suppose not.'

To tell the truth, we all gradually became fascinated with the entire absurd, quixotic project. How could anyone possibly hope to capture the atmosphere of a community life in an afternoon and evening? No matter, Walter and Hal and their helpers were completely confident that they could, and, by God, they seemed to be doing their damndest. They were here, there, and everywhere with their cameras, shooting everything conceivable: Demelza, Pacifist Pete, Isolde and her retinue, including, of course, Elbow and Ankle and Hywel and Greta and Harriet – they all got into the act. There were shots of Jesus meditating up a tree, and shots of another man doing yoga by the waterfall; shots of the woodcarver carving and of the potter potting; and shots of workers tilling in the fields while the womenfolk cooked around a communal fire. There were minor interruptions, as when one of the film unit knocked over a beehive and loosed a furious swarm, and again when the sound technician was suddenly chased into the creek by Elbow and Ankle, but the filming went relentlessly on. I learned from Demelza that Walter, believed in shooting thousands of feet of film, and later on extracting the few hundreds he wanted.

'Just think, Dad, all this will be on film.'

As she spoke, Demelza waved her hand expressively around at what, in a short period of a few months, had unexpectedly become our home. I looked around, with some surprise at my own sense of satisfaction. Truth to tell, I was just beginning to get used to it. There could be no doubt the setting *was* rather beautiful: the waters of the creek, the tall trees, the distant fields. And I had Demelza to thank for it all, yes indeed.

Affectionately, I put an arm round her shoulder.

'Well, who'd have thought it, eh? You and me ending up here in the Old Sawmills. My word, there's a busy future ahead of us!'

The filming went on and on, into the evening, into the night. The film unit, wise in their ways, had brought with them not merely the instruments of their trade but also a whole caseful of champagne. Liberally supplied with cardboard cartons of this potent stuff, the members of the Cornish Commune gradually assembled around the creekside, more than willing to

put on a really lively show. I had to admit I was a little
startled by the numbers – I must have counted nearly twenty.
I felt sure that Demelza and I had agreed on a quota of no
more than twelve. I decided, very firmly, that I would speak
severely to Demelza the next day.

As darkness fell, there was an added magical touch – a gentle
midsummer moon hanging low over the trees and reflected in
the water.

'Say, wouldya believe that?' said Hal almost in ecstasy.

The spot-lights were fixed on to the lawn, and there the
members of the commune happily did whatever was asked of
them. There were communal discussions and communal
debates and communal chanting and communal music and
finally, arms linked, communal dancing. All this, I am sure,
Hal captured with his special Japanese wide zoom camera, and
Walter no doubt got one of the others to intersperse shots of
the moonlit waters and distant shimmering woods, the entire
scenery of a magical world.

Indeed, as the champagne-flavoured evening went on and
on, and even Jess and I could not resist gently joining in such a
truly fantastic occasion, I think it became difficult for anyone
present *not* to believe in a marvellous manifestation of the true
brotherhood of man. After all, I told myself, sipping
enthusiastically my third or perhaps my fourth or fifth glass of
champagne, wasn't it really a wonderful thing that all these
very different people, instead of warring with one another,
were gathered together here in a kind of loving kindness,
forming a real communion of human beings?

I have vague memories of a night that seemed to go on for
ever ... of at some stage putting my benevolent arms around
Walter's broad shoulders and congratulating him, and then,
not wishing to appear rude, stretching up high to do the same
to Hal ... of joining hands with black-bearded Jesus in doing a
mock Russian folk dance which, for all I know, may have been
recorded for underground posterity by the whirling cameras
... and then there was a gay crescendo of activity when some of
the more lively of the beautiful people dragged old tree trunks
down to the water, mounted them, and paddled themselves out

into the creek to indulge in hilarious mock sea-battles, inventing a kind of water-dodgems war that ended in shrieks of laughter as everyone finally fell into the water.

It was magic, sheer magic, and at one stage I felt I wanted to say so to the instigator of it all. I found her, in a quiet moment, sitting staring pensively at the marvellous reflection of the moon in the water, and I put a friendly, if rather drunken, arm around her slim shoulders.

'Thou art – hic – Demelza, my daughter, in whom – hic – I am – his-well pleased,' I said, or words to that effect. And I went on muddledly repeating what I suppose must have been said rather often: 'You know, some time you and I must have a long, long, *very* long talk.'

'Sometime,' said Demelza. She suddenly squeezed my arm affectionately. But it was one of those moments of such indefinable accord that I like to think we both realized it was hardly necessary.

After that, somehow, the whole evening became submerged by a welter of sounds, of music and singing and shouting. Someone, Stephen probably, lit a huge bonfire and the flames rose higher and higher into the sky, so that God alone knows what demented visions crowded the narrow minds of our distant disapproving neighbours. The night went on and on and on … until, in the small dark hours of the morning, Jess and I fumbled our way up to our bedroom and fell into a deep, deep sleep.

V

The Crafts in Cornwall

In an area of such antiquity and timelessness as Cornwall, where indeed to feel this sense of past one has only to place the palms of the hands against some smooth worn shape of granite, it is perhaps only natural that crafts have always flourished. Craftsmanship has been described as the gradual transfer of the bodily knowledge of the right usages of material and the intimate co-operation of small groups of workers. If the continuity is broken and the workers and their materials split up then not only is a craft lost but often a whole heritage. During the last world war there was a very real danger of craftsmanship dying out but fortunately quite the opposite has happened and there has generally been a tremendous revival of interest in the art and craft of making things by hand.

Nowhere has this been more striking than in Cornwall where there are now about 500 separate crafts in existence. Some of these, such as the painting of sea shells and the making of fancy jewellery and decorations, are somewhat superficial and intended mainly for the tourist trade. However the interesting thing, about most of the crafts practised in Cornwall is that they are very old and very traditional – the crafts of the blacksmith, the wheelwright, the saddler, the coppersmith, the weaver, the potter. Among exponents of these crafts have been some of the best known members of their profession not only in Cornwall but in Britain: Bernard Leach, the potter, Francis Cargeeg, the coppersmith, Robin Nance, the furniture maker, Percy Mitchell, the boat builder, Jeanne Stanley, the rushmaker, Gladys Haymer, the weaver. Some of these are now dead, but their pioneering work has been carried on by others to an impressive degree.

In Cornwall, too, there has been the important link with the Celtic past, from an era when craftsmanship reigned supreme. When we think, in more general terms, of Inca pottery, Negro wood carvings, Neolithic figurines and so forth, all giving visual significance to the ritual of birth, life and death, we should not forget there were master craftsmen of the Celtic world who bequeathed such treasures as the Battersea shield, the Ardagh chalice and the Tara brooch.

It was a curious, almost instinctive interest in their work growing out of his love for Cornwall and its history, that first encouraged Francis Cargeeg, one of Cornwall's greatest craftsmen of the twentieth century. He became fascinated in the rich legacy of Celtic art, the creativity of a race whose dominion stretched for a thousand years from the Black Sea to the western coast of Ireland, and whose artists and craftsmen gave to Europe a masterly abstract art of curvilinear and geometric ornament:

They excelled particularly in metal-work, and in hammered sheet bronze, which is copper with a little tin added, they found a medium that perfectly suited their instincts and achieved astonishing results in the technique of 'Embossing' designs which we now know as 'repousse'. Their designs were drawn by the flow of light on polished metal, which gave an elusive beauty of their oft-times flamboyant and bizarre forms. Thus Celtic metal work and hammered copper appeared as an ideal medium to interpret the spirit which lived in the scrolls, the spiral and trumpet motifs and the amazing patterns of knot work so beloved by the ancient artist craftsmen.

My interests went hand in hand with a certain artistic urge which sent me to an art school in the evenings and to the open air with easel and water colours whenever possible. In this pilgrimage a dream slowly took shape of devoting myself to the awakening of interest in Celtic art and to restoring the prestige of beaten copper as an art-form. The interest in Celtic art in the antiquarian coteries in Cornwall was almost nil, and the art schools a subject for distinctly 'sniffy' comments; whilst owing to the ease with which copper can be manipulated by the machine, the once lovely art of beaten copper had become degraded to the point of extinction and served but to brighten the ironmongery department and solve the problems of the seaside souvenir hunters. So I left the security of an engineering job up country, crossed the Tamar into my native land, and set myself the task of literally hammering out a new pattern of life and making a distinct contribution to the Celtic revival of Cornwall.

My tribute has been by hand, hammer and fire to try to make a living reality of a great traditional art. My experience has brought me an acute sense of fellowship with my forerunners, and a satisfaction in sharing in the significant and inevitable revival of the crafts. Significant because it is part of that questing for those basic aesthetic values which, hag-ridden by the analytical spirit of a scientific age, the artist bewilderingly seeks. Inevitable because all they seek has been part of the way of life, labour and thought of artist craftsmen since the dawn-cultures of mankind. Hence the haunting of the studios, the hopeful drawing together of the artist and craftsman, the emergence of the artist craftsman of a new age.

Francis Cargeeg referred to what has been encouragingly evident in recent years: a vast return to, as well as a development of the crafts in Cornwall. The reasons for this are very much the same as apply to the painters and the poets and the writers – craftsmen (and women) too are similarly drawn to this unique world of surging seas, of white-washed sands, of craggy cliffs, of desolate moors and haunted interiors.

This aspect is very aptly summed up in the work of R.H. Cory who, working from his home at Widemouth, near Bude, has developed a strange and hauntingly beautiful craft in driftwood. What this gifted man does is wander around the coast of north Cornwall – beachcombing in fact – collecting all kinds of driftwood and then working on shaping them. He has found himself increasingly interested in the sources of the seawood, the relation of winds, currents and tides to the supplies of the raw material and so on:

> The techniques used to develop shapes from driftwood are matters of individual choice, as is the preference for tools. My own methods are essentially simple. I remove all bark, soft and rotted surface and faulty pieces by using files, chisels and a coping saw. There then remains the basic wood, which is obviously different in shape from the original piece. At this stage decision has to be made as to the ultimate shape required, so imagination and artistic sense come into play. The wood is viewed from all angles, regard being given to the grain and pattern and how they follow the curves, and account is taken of hollows and cavities and how best they may be used to enhance the completed model. Many pieces of driftwood contain very attractive colours, which are discovered only when the inequalities and blemishes of the exterior have been removed.
>
> Once when working on a piece of walnut root, I was thrilled to find black, orange and purple and an intermingling of colours impregnated into the basic colour of the wood. I discovered that any wood exposed to the action of sea water over a long period underwent two changes; one in colour and the other in texture. Changes in colour are due mainly to the dissolved mineral and chemical salts carried by the rivers into the oceans. Long immersion causes the wood to become infused with the salts.

Cory's is an especially vivid example of a particularly Cornish craft; one sees that the end product is literally alive with the feeling, the haunting presence, of the county of its creation. Where else, as Cory has said, except along the wild exposed sea coast of North Cornwall would he have found an intricately shaped piece of Canadian maple which he was able to carve into the shape of a ballerina? Or a piece of myrtle wood with infused black and orange colours which was eventually turned into a bird shape? Or again, specimens of bog oak, first mistaken for ebony, which he stumbled upon searching the pebble ridges of Millook, with its gigantic and magnificent folded strata cliffs towering majestically into the sky? And then there was an interesting example of nature aping life when Cory found a curved and twisted piece of gorse root, which had been swept into the ocean and returned to the shore, looking like a copy of Zadkin's famous commemorative monument standing in the middle of Rotterdam (i.e. the gorse root suggested the same experience of life, cruelty, torture, suffering, death, as Zadkin deliberately set out to achieve in his original carving).

Another Cornish craft that has grown greatly in popularity in recent years arises directly out of the nature of the county itself – namely the collecting and polishing and shaping of rare mineral stones. Cedric Rogers, one of the chief exponents, has pointed out that, like archaeology, stone collecting has a special significance for Cornwall. While there are other areas of Britain, notably Cumberland and Derbyshire, where minerals occur in some quantities, Cornwall is exceptionally rich. There are few places in the world of comparable size where so many different varieties (up to 300) are to be found. In the nineteenth century, when Cornish mining was at its peak, mineral collecting was a flourishing by-product. Fine crystals were continually being dug out with the rough ore. The miners would set aside the best specimens to sell to dealers, who, in turn, were kept busy supplying minerals to museums and private collections the world over. The output of at least one mine, whose ore was particularly well endowed with crystalline minerals, suffered because so much of it was boot-legged to dealers. The supply of such spectacular material has dropped in recent years, but collecting in Cornwall is still a very active hobby. Its devotees range from professors and their students, for whom mineral collecting is a practical extension of their studies, to amateurs, retired people, residents and weekending holidaymakers. To quote Cedric Rogers:

If you haven't been bitten by this particular collecting bug, you may wonder what the appeal is. One is unlikely to find any specimens like the beauties to be seen in museums, but with patience anyone can acquire a modest but attractive collection, with the odd rare specimen cropping up, which makes it especially worthwhile. It is also a *practical* hobby. The outlay is cheap, the bare equipment being a hammer and a magnifying glass; the materials are free; it takes one into the open air and supplies the incentive to exercise for those of otherwise lazy inclinations. On the other hand, it appeals to our romantic side. One's imagination is tickled with wild dreams of treasure hunting – for gold or precious stones. The discovery of crystals of some unfamiliar mineral is as exciting as finding a chest full of pieces-of-eight; anyone who has ever dreamed of being a prospector is already halfway to being a mineral hunter. It is also instructive and a jumping-off ground for more serious study. In Cornwall glamorous minerals abound – gold and silver beryl, topaz, zircon, garnet, turquoise, tourmaline, rhodonite, moonstone, perdot – and then the quartz family, amethyst, citrine, cairngorm, opal, agate, onyx, cornelian, chalcedony, jasper, praze, bloodstone. Cornwall is noted for its fine crystals of glass clear quartz – sometimes referred to as 'Cornish Diamonds' – as well as various other shades from white to black. The crystals are always six-sided, usually prisms ending in six-sided pyramids: small and slender or large and stumpy and stained brown with iron oxide.

The first thing that a would-be mineral collector must know apart from what to look for is where to look. The easiest and most natural place for the casual searchers in Cornwall is one of the dozens of beaches. Any one is a potential hunting ground, though some may produce only a monotonous repetition of the same kind of pebbles, but the beach at Marazion (opposite St Michael's Mount) has a wonderful variety of quartz and other pebbles which may contain the occasional amethyst or citrine. Other beaches may produce pleasant surprises of the same sort. Cliffs will often contain minerals which are easily visible, but hard to extract, since they form veins embedded in the solid rock;

but sometimes, with the patient use of a cold chisel and a heavy hammer, you may get some good specimens.

The serious mineral collector will waste no time in seeking out some of the old mine dumps. A drive through Cornwall will quickly reveal where the mine workings are grouped, and a rough rule to follow is that the greater the concentration of mines, the greater is the chance of a varied mineral concentration. The first area to head for in West Cornwall is that at Botallack, just north of St Just. If you find no interesting minerals, which is unlikely, you will be rewarded with some stunning scenery. A little to the north is Geevor tin mine, one of the only two mines at present operating in Cornwall. The second great mining area, even more extensive, is that extending eastward from Camborne to Redruth, Gwennap and beyond St Day; the other working mine, South Crofty, is located in the shadow of Carn Brea. North-east of this is St Agnes, with a smaller, but important concentration of mines, which extends to the east of Perranporth. The largest mining area in East Cornwall centres around Callington, once very active, and a key point for the collector now. Copper was mined here as well as tin, and occasionally silver; and interesting and rare copper minerals may still be found on some dumps.

Elinor Lambert was a craftsman who took the stone collecting habit one degree further. Around Mevagissey she would go out and search the beaches in a spirit of expectancy that was open and awake for a miracle, ready for any event, even – as has sometimes happened – the discovery of a familiar shape, a stone she threw back to the sea one dark night many months ago, slightly changed by the flux of the tides. Back on the floor of her cottage she would spread the stones out and looking at them would imagine past forms of the mighty spirit of forests, broken up and disintegrated, raw material for a new creation:

Now begins the fun. My stone and I get together intimately. I review it from all angles, almost always the figure I am chasing seems to be mysteriously cloaked in a shawl, a hood, or a cowl. My first attempts to emphasise by adding on were crude. Heads and hands had all the appearance of being stuck on; but with persistent self criticism, research and striving after texture and suitable colouring I arrived at a true marriage between my additions and the rock, sometimes modelling an entire torso emerging from a barnacled skirt. The making of one large figure is an elaborate and lengthy process. Additions are modelled on the stone, left to dry and shrink, and finally after several weeks to fall off. Then I start in with adherents (no drill will penetrate the stone) and after a further wait of several weeks pack into the join durable and weather-proof cement paints. The finishing textures are important both for their protective qualities and for their resemblance to the rock surface.

Working on a stone for an hour or so Elinor Lambert often found some chance lighting would bring a vivid sense that here was a character that once lived in history or had been created in literature. In this way she evolved such stone images as Shakespeare's Ophelia, Emily Brontë's Cathy, Socrates, Undine, the patriarchs of the Old Testament and others. Once she resurrected two little saints of her own town, Saint Meva and Saint Issey, the gull and the stream, who were said to have met here and given Mevagissey its name.

Living for any appreciable time on this strip of England which somehow is not really English one is caught in that strange net of influences of which the natives are unconscious because they are part of its fabric. It is secret, often sinister, and in league with the earth's dynamic centres. I have tried to catch the spirit of this, using a long rectangular stone as a wall and fashioning fishermen leaning on it, as they are in the habit of doing when they can't go to sea. There may be a row of them gossiping on that wall overlooking the harbour, but they are not with each other even in their talk. They are out there with their ships, suspended somewhere between the weather omens and the heaving tide that tugs at the wooden legs propped under the hulls. My fishermen have no faces, they are viewed from behind. You may speak to them and they will answer without turning. They speak to the bowl of the harbour.

Once the method and materials are mastered the scope of my work with stone is unlimited. So without end is it that while one may relax when contemplating the coves and beaches from the cliff top one is almost afraid to descend, to touch, to handle, to choose the individual stones, afraid because they all seem to wait to be chosen for reconstruction. Almost all have potential character, yet few can be brought to being as Stone People. The rest must be washed back with the tide till their time is come.

Wrought-iron work has always been a feature of Cornish life, where until recently at any rate every village had its own 'smithy'. Perhaps the best known exponent was the late Archibald Carne of Truro, whose exquisite traditional pieces won many prizes at important shows. He once recalled his early days, in the late nineties, when he grew up in a world of horses and carts, ploughs and harrows; that was when he first caught the fascination of a village forge, discovering that to watch a half a dozen or more big steaming horses waiting to be shod in the light of the forge fire while the smithy worked merrily and commandingly with red hot bars of iron was a thrill. Schooldays over he became apprenticed and learned the proper use of tools. However at the same time evening classes at Truro Art School in pencil work proved a useful parallel to the apprenticeship in hammerwork.

Later, after service in the war, a visit to the new world of India, and contact with all sorts of ideas and philosophies, Archibald Carne found that ordinary smithy work was not enough. He went back to art school and began tentatively copying natural forms of leaves and flowers in ironwork. Like the true and natural craftsman he was he began thinking that design in iron should surely bring out the characteristics of the metal itself, and so he began producing a beautiful range of wrought iron items – fires, log forks, candlesticks, screens, coal containers, mosaics. Especially he began to consider the full possibilities of iron in use and design, a place in a setting of modern architecture and life.

> Purpose and programme for a craft were forged at the anvil and brought out at the bench as well as with the pencil and book. Ideas for the piece, from the poker to the elaborate grate, made a contribution to the wider conception of what metal could do and what a smith could and should do with metal. The process was and is one of challenge and response in terms of craft, as in business practice it appears as demand and supply. But both are live factors. The settings of architecture, the problems of furnishing in our time are challenges to an ancient craft, heavy with tradition in working and design. How far can tradition be modified, discarded? How far can new designs or methods be created without loss of quality, the propriety that lies in the sense of metal? This, apart from love of tool work, is the exciting quest which the smith shares with modern members of other crafts. Where the smith like his fellow craftsmen has the main initiative he has the greatest freedom in conception. It is for this I have deliberately studied the designs of tradition to get what inspiration they might give either for development and adaptation or in rejection for the seeking of some new shape and line. But the study and work with the pencil must be tested and proved with the hammer to see again what iron may do and what place it may take in the world of changing styles, always to make the proper piece in its rightful place.

Looking back over a long life as a Cornish craftsman, Archibald Carne concluded that each craftsman within his range could make his contribution to the re-establishment and maintenance of his craft, not only in producing his work but also in continuing the ancient process of recruiting and bringing up in apprenticehsip new men, and to co-operate in willingness with local educational authorities – and this has been done at his forge and by many other craftsmen.

Rushwork is another interesting example of an old craft, revived in Cornwall in the 1950's by the late Jeanne Stanley. It all began for her one afternoon when she sat on a stool in a farmyard making a waste-paper basket out of direct rushes from the borders of the River Fal.

A neighbour passing by stopped and said: 'Did 'ee know that be an old, old Cornish job?' And he went on to explain how the old folk used to 'trace' the rushes and make them into maunds for field work – 'tracing' being plaiting or tressing the rushes, 'just like 'ee do trace a little maid's hair'. In the old days the rushworkers would take out pith and rub it in their hands to make the wicks for candles and fish-oil lamps. Farmers used rushes to thatch ricks, and housewives made mats for their blue stone floors.

At that moment rushcraft became alive for me. The only tools I wanted were sack needles, a ruler and sharp scissors. I could make baskets with no tools but my fingers as the American natives did. I had no textbook, but no book can teach as well as practical experience, and I have had plenty of that ... the vagaries of Cornish field rushes would fill a huge tome.

After that Miss Stanley searched into the history of Cornish rushwork, discovering that near Devoran, Falmouth, there was once a rush factory; that the Ancient Britons made rush baskets which were so admired by the Romans that they took them back to Italy (to this day Italians make rush trays in which to carry their fruit and vegetables); and that at one time Cornish children used to make their toys out of rushes, tiny baskets being favourites. Using all this knowledge Miss Stanley developed her unusual art, and before her death was awarded the title of *Gwyadores Bronnennow* ('Weaver of Rushes') at the Cornish *Gorsedd*.

Weaving in general has enjoyed a notable revival in Cornwall, where there is a flourishing Cornwall Guild of Weavers, whose secretary, Margery Hicks, has kindly supplied me with details of some of her members' activities. For instance, one of the best traditional weavers not only in Cornwall but in England had her workshop at Pontewan, near Mevagissey – Gladys Haymer, renowned for her samples of fine silk, woven on a dobby loom, that have the elegance of eighteenth century French brocade. Studios like hers, and Jennifer Angove's near Crantock, where the weaver can be seen working at the loom, seem immensely attractive to craft-hungry tourists.

The Roseland area of Cornwall is the home of several weavers – at Portscatho and at Veryan and at St Mawes, while not far away at Helston, an ex-Army officer, John Madden, built up Tweenstream Weavers and proved that anyone bold enough to enter into open competition with mass production can do so. Over at Praze, a retired engineer harnessed the power of an old water mill to drive his loom, and there are many other fascinating workshops to be found down remote Cornish byways, like the sail-loft workshop of a retired London bank manager near Port Isaac.

Finally, mention must be made of that gifted designer, Wyn Evans of Boligney, whose wall hanging 'hebula', a striking conception woven from aluminium strips on a ground work of fiery starlets, was bought by the Victoria and Albert Museum. Wyn Evans is one of the most exciting craft workers in Cornwall – particularly in her wall hangings such as 'Tresco', in which scimitar shapes of eucalyptus leaves from the gardens of Tresco Abbey on Scilly, are punctuated by dark blobs of bark picked up on St Agnes Beach and held in a shimmering web of muted plum and gold and grey.

It was another friend of mine, an embroiderer, Erma Harvey James, being occupied in a craft close to weaving, who once gave to me one of the most impressive explanations of the effect that Cornwall can have on a craft worker. Her childhood was spent at Hayle, where she was always wandering along the famous 'three miles of golden sands' and she remembers how shells and seaweed and fierce frail wings seen against sand and sun-pierced water formed an unconscious bias towards a particular emphasis, a personal conception of reality, which emerged many years later with the recognition of the remote connection between these images and the texture of thread on linen. The past, she came to realise, was nothing less than a very real source of richness, indeed like buried treasure which having lain in silence and darkness suddenly becomes accessible.

Crafts are very much a normal and natural part of daily life in Cornwall. In many a small fishing port or village, in quite remote country areas, as well as in market towns, the visitor is likely to find some craftsman working away down a side street, whether it be a wrought iron forge at Lelant, a boatmaking yard at Penryn or Mevagissey, or a furniture making workshop like Robin Nance's at St Ives, or (as was the case some years ago) Guido Morris's unusual Latin Press Printing workshop on the Island, overlooking Porthgwidden Beach.

In fact, endless examples can be quoted of Cornish craftsmen at work. To conclude, one cannot do better than consider the phenomenal development of a particular craft which in many ways is perhaps the best known of all in Cornwall – pottery. There are, of course, historical reasons why this ancient craft is associated in particular with the county, for it was in the areas of mid-Cornwall and North Cornwall and North Devon that William Cookworthy first made his original discoveries of ball-clay which led to the development of such a major industry. And with clay being mined in the area it was perhaps only natural that small potteries should start up. In fact raw clay was to be found in various parts of the county a long time ago and can still be dug up in such areas as St Hilary or St Erth, where the old clay-mines remain.

Today, the number of studio potteries at work in Cornwall is quite remarkable – at the last count the figure was nearly 100, and increases every year. It is certainly most unlikely that any other English county has a half or probably even a quarter of that figure. In Stoke-on-Trent, of course, there are many active commercial potteries, but that is really a different industry, and the difference between it and the studio potteries such as those found in Cornwall has been well put by a leading exponent on the latter:

The artist craftsman should be the natural source of

contemporary applied design, whether he works in conjunction with industry or prefers, as most of us do, to carry out our ideas in clay, cotton, wood, glass, metal or leather, etc., mainly with our own hands and at our own tempo. The hand is the prime tool and it expresses human feelings intimately; the machine for quantity, cheapness and, at best, a marvellous efficiency, but it turns man into a modern slave unless it is counterbalanced by work which springs from the heart and gives form to the human imagination.

When Bernard Leach wrote those words he could well have been thinking of developments over the past thirty years of the Cornish studio potteries – and indeed the Leach pottery at St Ives in particular. Founded in 1920, the pottery still occupies the same premises, at the top of The Stennack. Until 1937 the ware was fired in an old-fashioned wood kiln, but this has since been replaced by oil-burning kilns that produce a wide range of high-fired stoneware 'because it suits the conditions of modern life best and offers a wider field of suggestion and experiment'.

Not surprisingly the Leach Pottery and the distinguished reputation of its founder – and subsequently his sons, David and Michael Leach and his wife Janet – drew many followers. From the beginning a deliberate policy of taking students was adopted, while in addition short courses are held periodically for art students. Altogether more than 1,000 students must have passed through the pottery, so that its influence has been considerable. The co-operative side of the venture was always very important to Bernard Leach, who was himself trained in Japan, home of the co-operative pottery movement. He once said:

At the Leach Pottery, by accepting the Cornish motto of 'one for all and all for one' and by making the workshop a *we* job instead of an *I* job, we appear to have solved our main economic problems as hand-workers in a machine age, and to have found out that it is still possible for a varied group of people to find and give real satisfaction because they believe in their work and in each other. To me the most surprising part of the experience is the realisation that – given a reasonable degree of unselfishness – divergence of aesthetic judgement has not wrecked this effort. When it comes to the appraisal of various attempts to put a handle on a jug, for example, right in line and volume and apt for purpose, unity of common assent is far less difficult to obtain than might have been expected.

Bernard Leach believed strongly that the educated craftsman of today is thrown up as a reaction against the over-mechanisation of labour at a certain stage following the Industrial Revolution, and that this kind of person possesses an insight into the epochs of man's culture and in his or her own workshop passes such influences through the mesh of personality. And he believed equally strongly that Cornwall, a unique place, offers a unique opportunity for craftsmanship to flourish.

The Leach Pottery has by no means been the largest concern of its kind in Cornwall – there were two studio potteries in Newlyn alone (The Celtic Pottery and the Troika Pottery) that perhaps employed more people – but it is true to say that the Leach influence has drawn many potters to Cornwall. This does not mean that copying has been slavish; for instance, stoneware is not all that common, and most of the Cornish potteries produce earthenware pots.

The visitor will not travel far without finding a studio potter at work. Here are just a few of them: The Tintagel Pottery in Sir Richard Grenville's old home at Bossinney; Michael Cardew's stoneware pottery at Wenlock Bridge, near Bodmin Moor; John Nash's pottery at Marazion, overlooking the wide sweep of Mount's Bay, and nearby looming mass of St Michael's Mount; the Celtic Pottery and the Troika Pottery, both in former fish-cellars at Newlyn; Little Penderleath Pottery up on the moors at Nancledra, between Penzance and St Ives; the Polperro Pottery at the entrance to that famous and picturesque fishing port; the Millstream Pottery overlooking beautiful Fowey Harbour; John Vaisey's Modern Pottery near Truro; John Buchanan's Pottery at Halsetown. Several potters may also be found in the Craft Market St Ives, one of several similar concerns which have recently developed in Cornwall, adding still further to a pleasant atmosphere of craftsmen at work.

Far from the hustle and bustle of the big cities, in a world where artists are taken for granted and accepted as a natural part of the landscape, the potters of Cornwall have learned to appreciate their good fortune. It is seldom that a potter ever leaves Cornwall; though, contrariwise, not a year goes by without another handful making the trek west, searching for that old barn, that former fish-cellar or some similar building suitable for converting into a pottery. This, indeed, is the trend among all crafts, for the Rural Industries Bureau confirms that more and more such people are moving into Cornwall. Not only is this one invasion that might surely be welcomed, for a change; it is a simple yet impressive proof of the scope that mysterious net in which Cornwall seems to enmesh all kinds of creative workers.

VI

Wining and Dining

Cornwall being a major tourist centre it would be surprising if it did not contain quite a few memorable hotels and restaurants. Living as we do in the county we have less occasion to visit these than the holidaymaker; nevertheless over the years we have become familiar with a fair number. I have no means of knowing what the general standard of service is in Cornwall, but I can speak with experience of certain establishments.

One that Jess and I always remember with some nostalgia is the Tregenna Castle, whose striking buildings stand high above St Ives. The reason for the nostalgia is that very early in our married life I landed a useful little commission to write a brochure for the Tregenna, a project which included a free weekend's stay. What a contrast that made with our tiny cottage on the side of Trencrom – suddenly we were transplanted into a world of thick rugs and wide, wide corridors (the main entrance corridor at the Tregenna, we discovered, was nicknamed 'Scandal Alley'!)

There were tennis courts and squash courts and a large swimming pool and a luxury cocktail bar and we availed ourselves of all these luxuries – especially enjoying wandering about the beautifully kept sloping lawns with their breathtaking views over picturesque St Ives and its bay, with Godrevy standing white on the horizon. It was a different view of St Ives to our normally more intimate one, and none the worse for that, and we thoroughly enjoyed our weekend – after which I retired to our two-roomed cottage and duly wrote a glowing brochure.

Another St Ives hotel we had occasion to come to know was the Porthminster, the next biggest to the Tregenna, but set much closer to the sea – indeed standing right over it above Porthminster beach. Once again we were not in the habit of staying at anywhere like the Porthminster – it just happened to be the setting for the annual Penwith Society of Arts' Ball, an annual red letter day in our social calendar. Usually a particular theme would be chosen, and for the evening the vast ballroom would be suitably transformed, by many willing artistic hands – thus into a desert island, if the theme was pirates. These were always very gay occasions and somewhere I have a faded photograph of us all in fancy dress – myself as the Queen of Sheba!

It was good to see so many old friends at a single occasion – Peter Lanyon and Johnny Wells, Terry Frost and Willy Barns Graham, Bernard Leach, Barbara Hepworth – come to think of it, quite a distinguished list. Those were the immediately post-war years, when the new Penwith Society was full of exciting and progressive talent, and this was usually reflected in some very ambitious tableaux produced for the ball. Prizes were a simple matter – paintings by well-known painters, or some pots by Bernard Leach or perhaps exquisite woodwork by Robin Nance.

In a very different part of Cornwall – the wealthy resort of St Mawes opposite Falmouth on the south coast – we came to know the Idle Rocks Hotel simply because Zofia Ilinska, wife of the proprietor, was a famous poet and regular contributor to my *Cornish Review*. As she once wrote:

We provide the expected Pub, the usual Barber, Baker and coffin maker
The usual female persons prepared to marry
Bearded men in charge of steamers, hooting in harbours,
Shaggy men in rubber boots magnificent with oars,
Cleanshaven men drying yards of netting,
Several burnt by the wind, mostly fishermen.
We specialise in the smell of seaweed;
In the introvert seabirds absorbed in marine vegetation;

In high stepping waders patrolling the estuary.
Endlessly assaulting pallid molluscs.

Jess and I often visited Zofia at her gracious house standing high above St Mawes, a place of great peace and relaxation, where she wrote such marvellous poetry. However, for her, everyday life really took place down in the long green-shuttered hotel on the edge of the water. Once for the *Cornish Review* Zofia wrote me fascinating extracts 'From a Cornish Hotelier's Diary', and some of them seem well worth quoting as giving an insider's view of just what goes on:

'Saturday morning. They are all here now, the new arrivals, except for one honeymoon couple stranded off Jamaica Inn. They are all here: The doctor and the progress-chaser; the hospital matron and the anaesthetist; the stockbroker and the dress designer; the nice man, with the strong smell of Eton; the woman with a passion for delicatessen; the jittery, nerve-racked, unable-to-relax tycoon; the portrait painter, scrutinising faces; the mother of the species enquiring about safe beaches; the venerable arch-deacon, the deserted duchess; the long-long-married experts in fidelity, and the person switching spouses on and off like lights, gaily introducing her brand-new husband. They are all here: the hewers of wood, the drawers of water, the workers in cement; the good mixers – mixing; the bad ones hiding behind sheets of the *Western Morning News*. A few communing with lapdogs ... And others – now settling on the dining room banquettes to peruse the menu, which – in French and English – explains what in the way of food this house has to offer.

'What about Cornish fare, since this is Cornwall? Kiddley broth of marigold heads and finely-chopped 'scifers'? Muggety pie of calf's cord boiled then baked with onion and sauce? Stargazy pie, with herring, pilchard or mackerel, heads and tails protruding from the pastry? Scrowled pilsher, grilled on red hot coals with salt and butter on top? Herb beer with yeast fermented?

'Mysterious recipes out of reach of the average tourist, who –
if curious enough – may still succeed to get an inkling into how
the people of this sea-swept land used to live and eat. The
teddy oggy, no doubt, will soon offer itself to you and the figgy
hobbin, perhaps, and the clotted cream and the saffron cake.
You may come across curious notices in shop windows,
illustrating former customs, old signboards in curiosity shops
advertising 'lemanade and gingur-beer, cow hels and tripe
every friday, Sekond hand cloes to make ee tidy crox and
kittles, pans and all and Godly bukes to save yer sole, man
traps, gins and pattens likewise and on Saturday nights hot
mutton pies.' You may hear of young squabs, cormorants or
plucked curlews in pies, but it is unlikely that you will ever taste
them. Offered the choice of lobster from Porthleven, crab
from Newlyn, salmon from the Torridge, sole, turbot, brill,
mussel or scallop from Billingsgate, you will feel appreciative,
outlandish, in touch with Cornwall and the submarine life of
her seas.

*

'Saturday – 8 p.m. – dinner – service not bad. The subdued
sounds of a full dining room. Snatches of conversation: 'What,
no scampi, Luigi?' 'Mummy,' asks a child at the top of his
voice, 'what is this blue?' – 'What blue, where?' – 'The purple
lady with the horrid blue on the tops of her eyes.' 'What do
you do here in the winter?' insists the voice in what looks like
mink. Someone talks of delivering babies. 'She did it by her
own steam, no Caesar.' Someone enquires about the chough,
that Cornish bird. 'Only two pairs left, sir, one in the Zoo. On
the point of extinction, they say, disapproves of the tourist.'
Someone at the window-table would like background music.
'We employ the seagull, Madam, for that specific purpose. On
duty most of the time providing it.'

*

'Cocktail Bar. A small crowd has gathered in here around
Boudad, the cocktail expert. Soft lights, soft seats, soft music,
soft and not soft drinks. Little paper flags flutter round the
ceiling, wallpapered to look like the starry sky. High stools,

glass tables worked in wrought iron, anemones under the glass of each. 'I water them with whisky and gin,' says Boudad. Bottle shapes, chunks of ice, olives green and black, apple peel, orange peel, rind of the lemon. Sugar made shining and green sticks to the rim of the glass, tongue licks and licks, straws make funny sipping noises. 'This is the Yellow Submarine Cocktail. I serve it to honeymooners.' A cherry bobs up and down. Peanuts and short drinks, witticisms and laughter; gin and pink and someone sad among the bar stools and a mouth-smacking and splashing in Pimms No 1, and someone vacant listening to nothing. Midnight already, and Sunday. Outside the sea carries on its vast orchestral effects.

*

'Sunday, 5 a.m. – and the first seagull emits a bullying wail. The bay is full of ships sheltering from the storm. All lit up – very beautiful. In the kitchen quarters a voice picks up the refrain of a pop-song, then the first hoover, the tinkling of morning teas.

*

'Bright sun – sudden transition to this most marvellous of mornings, with the gulls hurrahing in the sky, the porters sweeping last night's sea away and everywhere the lovely, clean, rain-washed look. The beach is strewn with flotsam and jetsam, like a room after a party – with one solitary high-heeled shoe, size number five, incongruously poised on a rock. Some vanished Cinderella ... There's a heatwave in the air, I can feel it in my bones, and now that the sea is calm, the boats reappear. I ask two very young friends, experts at rowing, to reconnoitre the harbour. They bring the following report:

'*Demelza*, the big white boat, with a man in pyjamas abroad. He must have stayed the night aboard, because he would not have rowed out in pyjamas. *Anguilla*, blue motor boat. *Ratona*, green sailing boat, 18 ft long. *La Bamba*, big white French sailing boat, washing out underwear and trunks. *Careema*, a big blue motor boat, made in Falmouth. *Heidi*, large sailing boat, motoring about, saying '*bonjour*' to people about *La Bamba*. And *Felicity* Z1 and *Memory* Z17, and others of every description. The sea is alive with sails, white, rusty and blue.

The Customs boat appears, patrols up Percuil River. A day for spinnakers. Shall we sail? Shall we race? Come on, skipper! Keep me a lobster. Will you crew for me? What do you know about ropes, and tides and the hoisting of sail?

'Off the lighthouse the four tugs hang round waiting. For what? A tanker? A liner?

*

'Late morning – and the sea front crowded – the usual holiday crowd. Women in slacks and windcheaters, nondescript men sucking ice cream, windswept youths in bright yellow life jackets; Wellington boots, beach shoes, flip-flops; sound of flip-flops on the wet pavement; bare heels, pink heels, pebbly heels; long hair against brown rock; lollipops, towels, bikinis, long sweaters over bikinis; jeans, shorts, rugs on beaches; transistors in the sand, bottles of suntan oil, dogs uprooting centipedes, centipedes invading picnic baskets; vagabonds invading the village: 'They are sleeping rough,' says the postman. 'I saw them on the rocks the other night. Had a fierce fight near Holy Well, blood flying.' The village calls them 'black feet.'

*

'Paddling voices of children across the water. One with a yellow bucket – asks me to visit him. 'No 5, in London, but the number has fallen off the gate.'

The weather lures you out to explore 'vanishing Cornwall.' And what, what do you know of Cornwall? Does it really vanish?

I know that it is the land of the tourist; land of seabird and rock; the tidal estuary and the mining of tin; the lobster pot and the fish net drying; the surfing beaches and the drowning people; the Duchy Ball at the Headland and the foghorn voice everywhere; the ghoulies and the ghosties; the boats sailing into changing light and changing wind; the pirates of the days gone by; the ships, the shipwrecks, the spinning of yarns; the Cornish pasty, 'zacly the proper shape' – and whatever that man Lawrence wrote about this land.

*

'I like Cornwall very much. It's not England. It is bare and dark and elemental – Tristan's land – bare and sad under a level sky. It is old, Celtic, pre-Christian. Tristan and his boat and his horn. The Cornish people still attract me. They have become detestable, I think, and yet they aren't detestable. They are, of course, strictly anti-social and un-Christian. But then, the aristocratic principle of magic to which they belonged, these two have collapsed and have left only the most ugly, scaly, insect-like, unclean selfishness. Nevertheless, the old face is still revealed; a race which believed in the darkness, in magic and in the magic transcendency of one man over another. ... Also there is left some of the old sensuousness of the darkness, a sort of softness.

*

'A true picture? I have come to find out – and you, and you, and you – collecting picnic lunches from reception office, loading your rugs, your maps, your binoculars into the ever-loving car, ear cocked to the call of a distant creek, you hasten to catch the quarter-to or the quarter-past-the-hour King Harry Ferry.

*

'And there are other pastimes described on the blackboards invitingly propped up against the sea wall. Study us.

"What can be sweeter than a trip with Peter? A short cruise? A longer cruise? – 'Percuil River, St Anthony, Place Monastery, leaving the Ferry steps at 11 a.m. Tickets at pier gate, adults 5/-. *White Chief* – Cruise the beautiful Fal River to Malpas, viewing lovely creeks and caves. Toilet on board. Twelve seats only.' 'If you want to go fishing for mackerel, pollock, bass, etc., see Sonny. Rods, handlines and bait supplied.' *'Blue Bell* – cruise to Helford River, Frenchman's Creek, viewing Manderley from *Rebecca*, Port Navas and other places. 10/-.' 'The Absolute End in Orgies Tonite on the Castle

Beach. Bangers and other Delicacies laid out. Organised by You Know Who.'

*

'Lazily loitering in the harbour, in unhurried, snow-white spendour, seven swans. They have the oddest way of hitching up one black foot on the top of their backs like a dark rubbery shopping basket. are they left-handed? It is always the left one which is hitched-up. Six out of seven have done it. The seventh ruffles himself with anger, hissing. They treat him with aloofness. On the sun-terrace – to and fro – a tiny turnstone rushes on orange feet. 'The young of the seagull,' explains a man from Notting Hill Gate. 'But he does not look like the seagull,' protests his companion. 'Why should he? The gull, too, must have been young once.'

*

'The couple in Room No. 7 are planning to buy a house: 'On the sea front, for our retirement. Could we settle here, be happy, get used to the climate, get on with the locals, become Cornish one day? How does one do it?

'Slow, uncertain process. But – in time – you may qualify if you are lucky, learn to converse with boats and buoys, catch your mooring without visible panic, attend gorsedds, secure your dinghy, handle oars properly, learn secrets concerning tides, currents, reef knots, splices; fall into the harbour, fall into love of a Cornish person, avoid cocktail parties, climb a hundred slippery stones to attend herons nesting, hear things that go bump in the night, be kind to strangers, say "hullo" nicely, learn about saffron, sing in a choir, help one another; if you really try not to be proud, thoughtless, a bully, pompous, selfish, wishy-washy,sheepish, a snob ...

'Most important of all – if Cornwall gets to love you, decides to adopt you. And that depends on yourself ...'

When we lived at the Old Sawmills, Golant, we used to sometimes call in at the huge Fowey Hotel, looking out over the beautiful harbour, but it always seemed rather staid, and

full of retired couples. During this time, too, we had occasion
to stay at the Falmouth Hotel, but this was a happier occasion,
one of the annual West Country Writers' Conferences of which
I have written in earlier books. On this occasion the guest of
honour was C.S. Forester, creator of Hornblower, who turned
out to be a mild and shy man. It was good to meet lots of old
friends like Henry Williamson and Winston Graham and John
Bayliss and Derek Stanford and J.C. Trewin, another
Cornishman. This was another of those huge and luxurious
hotels, not high on character, but pleasant for a literary
weekend. I wonder if this was the time when Henry was in a
particularly mischievous mood, flicking rolled up pellets of
bread at various distinguished people ...

Nearer at home we have the Queen's in Penzance, standing
four square on the front and looking out upon our most lovely
Mount's Bay. Then there is the Old Success at Sennen Cove;
now there's a marvellous position, just a few yards from
the magnificent surfing beach – oh, yes, when I think about it
Cornwall has some pretty good hotels, especially site-wise.

Restaurants can offer variety, too. As readers of my books
may remember I have my own favourite of all, and that is
Enzo's, a first class Italian restaurant to be found, improbably,
in a tiny village about three miles out of Penzance, on the
lonely road to St Just. If we want a truly memorable evening,
both gastronomically and socially, then Enzo's is where to go.
However there are other restaurants, some with much more
exotic settings – the Count House, for instance, close by
Botallack Mine, that strange and eerie wilderness cut into the
side of the cliffs. The restaurant stands in what was literally
once the mine's count house, and is well worth a visit.

On the other side of Penwith, bang in the centre of
Mousehole, there is a popular restaurant whose eating area
stands on stilts right out into the snug little harbour – you
won't get many better viewpoints, especially if the harbour
gates are open and some Cornish fishing boat comes steaming
in.

A similar but larger view of harbour life can be found at the
Smuggler's Rest at Newlyn – for this is the second biggest

fishing port in the West of England and always bustling with life. I have always loved Newlyn, with its genuine working atmosphere, its constant panorama of long lines of fishing boats – many of them brothers and sisters to our dear old *Sanu*. Possibly my favourite occupation on a sunny day is to park the car by the fish market and then stroll along the outer quay, glancing down at one exciting boat after another. There used to be one that was indeed a identical companion to *Sanu*, called *Karenza*, but unfortunately in recent times it caught fire at sea and had been a total loss, though fortunately without any injuries to the crew who were promptly taken off by another boat.

In Penzance there are restaurants of course, plenty of them, ranging from the snug little Bistro to the larger Bosun's Locker, from Maggie Fisher's health food restaurant in Causewayhead to the vegetarian restaurant in Market Jew Street – while down by the harbour is the elegant Le Tarot, whose mosaics were made initially by our dear friend Llewellyn Baker. And then there's St Ives – The Outrigger and the Bistro and the Blue Haven, plenty of choice there.

Yes, in Penwith we are lucky in our restaurants (there is even an original and very good Spanish one over at Hayle, just beyond the causeway) and we are certainly not lacking in the means for a pleasant evening out.

VII

The Winter's Tale

Recently salvaging through some old cine films we came across several taken in our early days as owners of our old MFV *Sanu*. One in particular brought back many nostalgic memories, for it was a film not of one of our many trips, but of the comparative humdrum pace of a winter 'lay up'. In those days, of course, we lived at St Ives, but we could not have kept a boat like *Sanu* in that exposed harbour for a whole winter – no, we had to find somewhere rather safer.

Obviously there was only one possible place, and that was Hayle Estuary across St Ives bay, where most of the St Ives fishing boats put in, even during the summer. Once, Hayle had been a very busy port, but the existence of a sand bar across its entrance had been partly responsible for a decline in trade. There was still a regular traffic of coal and scrap boats which came in on one tide and usually left on the next after unloading. Most of these large boats followed the narrow channel that wound up past the big electricity works and into the town of Hayle itself, where there were commercial wharves.

However, about a couple of hundred yards inside the sand bar there was a fork in the river, and the narrow right-hand channel led up to an old disused quay known as Lelant Quay. Like St Ives harbour, this quay dried out at low tide, but the bottom was reasonably flat, with a mixture of shingle and sand, and there was room alongside for several large boats. Unlike Hayle it was not on the farther side of the river, but on the St Ives side, and no more than ten minutes by car from our house.

Here, then, we decided to make *Sanu*'s winter home. We had

moored sometimes at the quay during the summer and knew that it was seldom used because the fishing boats preferred to go into Hayle where they could unload their catch direct to waiting lorries. When we brought *Sanu* over from St Ives we assumed that we would have the quay to ourselves, and it was momentarily disquieting, as we crept slowly between marking posts, up the very narrow channel, to spy the masts of two other ships already moored there.

Naturally they had chosen the best positions, and there was nothing for us to do but cautiously edge our way rather farther up than we had been before. We tied up above the second of the boats, a MFV like ours belonging to a Lamorna man who, we later learned, had been half way round the world in her. This was *Flowing Tide* – the other boat was one of the best-known St Ives fishing boats, the *Sweet Promise*, which was having a refit.

Once tied up at the quay we put down our outside leg, made sure that we had plenty of old car tyres lining the side against the quay, and went off home. The next day I came back at the time of low tide just to check up that *Sanu* was settling down reasonably well. It was just as well I did – for I found our beloved boat tilting away from the quay at an alarming angle, only saved from toppling over by the one sturdy leg!

What had happened was that, while the bottom around the quay was flat at the seaward end, farther up it shelved away so that in fact there was no flat surface for the leg to rest on, and it only touched ground after tilting down some distance. If we had not put out a leg, the boat would have gone over on its side.

Nothing could be done until the tide came in again. I went home and collected Jess and our daughter Gill – unfortunately Stephen was away – and we drove back around high tide. My idea was that we would simply pull the boat back nearer to the other boats, as I had worked out that by so doing we would be back on the flat part. But I had underestimated the strength needed; we pulled and pushed and shoved, but the only result was the rather alarming one that having loosened the rear rope, *Sanu*'s flat bottom was swinging perilously out into mid stream. There was nothing for it but to start up the engine, with all those laborious procedures; and at last, with the aid of the engine, and Jess and Gill manoeuvring the ropes on the quayside, we managed to move *Sanu* back those vital few feet. We were rather near to the stern of *Flowing Tide*, but then, we noticed, she in turn was close on to the *Sweet Promise*: and in fact the three of us spent several quiet and trouble-free months moored in these positions.

Our first job, self-evidently, would be to clean and paint *Sanu*'s hull. When we had acquired her the Falmouth boatyard manager had congratulated us on our 'good bottom', but since then we had accumulated a formidable amount of weed and barnacles. I had never been quite able to comprehend that it is possible, but in fact the presence of these flimsy substances on the hull can knock a knot off the boat's speed. Well now, when the tide was out, it was easy to walk under the huge fat hull and the barnacles alone ran into hundreds. There was nothing for it but to drive across to the Fisherman's Co-operative at Newlyn and purchase several large cans of red anti-fouling paint and half a dozen scrapers.

Thus armed, one Sunday, we descended on the quay, along with several of Stephen's friends – the latter a great help, for we found that the children could get underneath *Sanu*'s hull without much trouble, whereas Jess and I could only reach it lying on our backs. The whole job was a painfully drawn-out one, for we were dealing with a hull sixty feet long and eighteen feet wide. First we had to pass down the hull with the scrapers, wearily hacking off the weed and barnacles. Then we had to go round with putty, looking for any possible cracks or crevices, though I was relieved to find the hull seemed in excellent condition.

Finally there came the onslaught with paintbrushes and the red anti-fouling – a tedious, seemingly never-ending task at the end of which, inevitably, we were almost as covered in paint as the boat. Still, miraculously, after two or three such visits, *Sanu*'s hull was finished, a gleaming rusty red – and free of weed and barnacles for some time to come.

Once the hull had been tackled, we did not feel so bad, as

the remaining work would at least be on board, and even if the weather stopped us painting there was plenty to do below deck. In fact, as it was autumn – a *Cornish* autumn, which can be quite heavenly – we were able to tackle painting the whole of the sides of the deck, and finally the deck itself. Previously it had been painted a light green colour, and since this would not really go with our planned blue and white exterior, we decided to paint the deck a rusty-red.

Our original intention was to use a material called Dekaplex, which is waterproof and gives weather protection to the cabins below. When we went to buy some they were out of stock, but they did have in some red lead paint of the same colour which they recommended. Much to our subsequent regret, to save wasting time Jess and I brought back two gallons of the stuff. It did not take us long to paint it on, and the resulting effect was most pleasing. Off we went, feeling very satisfied with ourselves ... only to return after three days to find, to our dismay, that the paint was still tacky and soft. We felt instinctively things were not as they should be, but went away and gave it another three days. When we came back, there was hardly any change.

Jess and I looked at each other in dismay.

'Supposing it *never* dries?' I said.

When we asked one or two supposedly knowledgeable friends they were even inclined to agree that this was a possibility, and our spirits sank to zero. We decided to make a great effort and leave the boat alone for two whole weeks. Meantime, I wrote off to the Dekaplex Company – and of course we soon realised what had happened. The previous Dekaplex surface was a plastic one, which admitted nothing, whereas paint usually soaks into the substance it is put on – the red copper was unable to do this!

Fortunately our worst fears were not realised. After two more weeks there was a slight but unmistakable improvement, and after that, resigning ourselves to the very slowest progress, we found that very gradually the paint did dry – so that after two months it could be said to have dried off. Finally we were able to apply the new coat of Dekaplex.

After that we turned our attention to the interior of *Sanu*. Ever since we had first acquired her we had felt very strongly that for a boat of her size the saloon was a little on the small size. We had enlarged it slightly by knocking down a partition to the galley, but we had found during the Channel Isles trip that the confinement could be irritating with a large party.

Adjoining the saloon was quite a large bathroom, an unexpected luxury on such a boat – and the fact was that no one had ever used the bath, for of course in the summer months everyone went swimming anyway. Naturally one could envisage times when a bath would be appreciated, but these did not seem sufficiently frequent to justify occupying such a large space.

"If we took away the bathroom the saloon would be half again as big,' pointed out Jess.

I was a little hesitant to embark on such an apparently destructive scheme, but finally agreed. We spent a busy afternoon tearing down the bathroom walls – and an even busier time manoeuvring the heavy cast-iron bath out of the cabin and up the narrow stairs to the wheelhouse. At one time there were five of us trapped in a seemingly impossible position half way up the stairs, but somehow in the end brute strength triumphed.

Now we entered what afterwards we termed our plumbing phase. To remove the bath and washbasin we had, of course, first to seal off the water connections. This meant taking up the floor boards as a result of which, apart from having a somewhat alarming view of the very bowels of *Sanu*, we were confronted by lengths of rubber piping running here, there and everywhere.

Gradually we managed to identify the various pipes, and cut off the important ones. Next we had decided in place of the bathroom to put a small sink in each of the three cabins. This seemed a simple enough operation involving merely the running of supply and waste pipes to each room, where we fitted in three small sinks bought in readiness. We joined the various pipelines with jubilee clips, connected up the water – and turned on the taps.

'Stop it!' we cried simultaneously. 'Shut off the water.'

Water was squirting out from almost every join we had made ... and now we learned a lesson of plumbing seared for ever into our minds. Check and double check and treble check every join – and then add putty! We found we had to start again from scratch, insert washers of squares of linoleum and tighten everything twice as tight as before – until at last we had the supply position in order. Then we had the same trouble over the waste pipes. Altogether I estimated we must have spent perhaps thirty hours over a job which probably an experienced plumber would have managed in three.

'Never mind,' said Jess wearily. 'It's one way of getting to know our boat.'

Gradually, over the winter months, I began to realise how true this was. Through tackling various jobs ourselves, willy nilly we became more knowledgeable about the intricate working of *Sanu*. Soon we had ripped up the linoleum in the saloon, alarmed to find the boards beneath dripping wet from the condensation – it was a pleasure to see them dry out and coat them with varnish. As far as possible we let the air get to every part of *Sanu*: meantime Jess and Gill were busy making fresh apricot-coloured hessian covers for the foam rubber seats in the saloon, which of course we had now extended to cover the area which had been the bathroom.

When all was finished we put down some plain Chinese matting, and felt reasonably pleased with our efforts. We had moved the diesel drip-through stove to one side, so that now we had a long L-shaped saloon big enough for a dozen people to relax in, in comfort. It was true, of course, that – mesmerised by the idea of expansion – I was beginning to suggest pulling down the double cabin and making the saloon even bigger, but Jess managed to restrain me. Instead we painted out the two front cabins, stripped the main beams of the saloon, painted the wheel-house again – and as a final domestic touch converted the two single bunks of our deck cabin into a more friendly double bed.

While busy with our interior decorating of *Sanu* I had not been forgetting the far more important matter of our engine –

or perhaps I should begin to say, engines. From the moment we had first bought *Sanu* we had always felt slightly uneasy about the fact that she only had the single, though admittedly powerful, Kelvin diesel. Apparently it is quite the custom up in Scotland for fishing boats to have only the single engine, and that should be recommendation enough, for there are no better boats and, potentially, no worse conditions for boating. On the other hand, I well knew that this was not by any means the custom in the West Country; where most of the larger fishing boats have two engines (our contemporary, *Karenza*, at Newlyn, had a main and a wing engine).

When I discussed the problem once with David Saqui, *Sanu's* previous owner, he made an expressive gesture. 'Don't worry. It's a magnificent engine, it'll get you home on one cylinder if necessary.' While first-hand experience had given me more and more confidence in our Kelvin, I could never rid myself of the unanswerable query – an engine *can* fail for a dozen reasons, and just *suppose* our engine did fail in circumstances where there was precious little time to do much about it? Supposing we were close to a rocky shore, with the tide carrying us in? We had no sails, and even if we had there might be no guarantee that they could get us out of such trouble. If, on the other hand, we had a second engine, even quite a small one, its presence might literally mean the difference between safety and disaster – even between life and death.

So, after a lot of humming and hawing, we had decided to order a second engine. Because we wanted an engine that was as uncomplicated as possible we chose an air-cooled type: a diesel of course, since these were obviously safest and most economical; and hand-starting to avoid any undue dependence on an electrical system. It was quite an education studying all the different catalogues and advertisements. For a time we toyed with the gamble of picking up a cheap second-hand engine, but in the end we felt that since this was a safety measure it was wisest to start from scratch and have a new engine.

Finally we plumped for a 36-horse power Lister and put an order through to the manufacturers in Gloucestershire. Mike

Peters, a St Ives marine engineer, agreed to handle the installation, with the help of his friend, Dick Pollard, a shipwright, and before Christmas came they had cleared away some of the ballast on the port side of *Sanu* and bored a hole through the beams ready for the stern-tube and shaft. These were ordered from a firm in Scotland, and were expected within a week or two. It was the engine, actually, that we were worried about: there was a ten-week period, as we understood, and that meant waiting until nearly Easter.

As it happened, we were lucky: word came through within two weeks that there was an engine ready, and rather than lose the opportunity Mike Peters drove to Gloucester and collected it in his van ... The next morning he called me round to his workshop, and there was the gleaming bright, gleaming new engine.

'We shan't be long now,' he said cheerfully. 'Soon as the stern tube comes we can get on with the job.'

That was at the beginning of January. A week went by; another week; and yet another week. I began to get anxious, and persuaded Mike Peters to ring up Glasgow. The answer was elaborate and apologetic, but the gist of it was that so far nothing had been sent. Another week passed ... and another. Now we were into February, and still no sign. More phone calls, more explanations. At one stage Mike Peters begged them to send just the tube, the rest later ... It seemed to make no difference. Another week of silence – *and one more week*!

At long last he came and phoned up for the sixth time from our house and both of us heard a solemn pledge from the other end that the goods were on the way by passenger train. And in fact at the very end of that week, on a Friday afternoon, the stern tube finally arrived ... just as Dick Pollard was due to start a two-week job that would prevent him doing any work for us! However, later that evening he and Mike Peters managed to get the stern tube installed, so that the shaft could be ordered, and the work was planned to be completed in a fortnight's time.

While waiting for the long-delayed stern tube I decided we might as well go ahead with a general check-up of our Kelvin engine. Like most of the big diesel engine makers, Kelvin's have a special service engineer for each district, and ours was the firm of Cowls, over at Porthleven. One crisp February day their chief engineer, Bill, drove over and I spent a couple of hours with him going through the engine's performance. I remembered that Doug had thought there was a bad lack of compression suggesting a worn piston or rings. So now when Bill nodded confirmation, I did not worry unduly, for I expected *some* repair work.

'Since I've got to take off that one,' he said, 'would you like me to check on them all? It's up to you.'

At first I was tempted to leave well alone, since the old Kelvin seemed to be functioning quite well. However, this wasn't like a car – it was a hundred times more important to avoid a mechanical breakdown with a boat than a car, which can just be taken to the nearest garage.

'Very well – go ahead.'

It was arranged that I should call back at the boat on the following afternoon to hear the verdict. At that time my mind was fairly preoccupied with other things, and anyway I had no particular reason to be apprehensive. Alas, I had hardly got down the ladder into the engine-room before one look at Bill's face struck a chill into my heart.

'Is it bad, then?'

It was; pretty well as bad as could be. Not only would he have to replace piston and liner on No 3 chamber, but in fact the other liners were worn – and worse, much, much worse, when he came to examine the cylinder heads, three of them had hairline cracks in them, which meant water was getting past.

Furtively I sorted out the Kelvin spares list and began looking up prices. One look was enough to make me groan: cylinder heads were £20 each, and this price list was five years old.

'Prices are up ten per cent on that,' said Bill apologetically.

Patently, there was nothing much else that could be done, but agree to the necessary work. There then began a curiously distasteful process of disembowelment – at one stage I came into the engine-room and it was rather like interrupting an operation at its most critical stage. Bits and pieces of my beloved Kelvin lay strewn all over the engine room ... and in the centre, where usually that shining brass-topped engine stood so proudly, there was only a broken shell. I could hardly believe my eyes – and I could certainly not believe that Humpty Dumpty would ever be put together again.

But he was. Bill was one of those born mechanics who have grown into their vocations; somehow his thick oily fingers worked with all the skill of a surgeon, above all he was patient, extracting piece after piece. It was no joke either, sometimes, for certain parts of the Kelvin weighed more than one man could carry, and we had to use a truck to wheel them away to Bill's van. However, somehow it was all managed, and after only a week or so, I came down the ladder one Friday midday to find Bill smiling quietly to himself – and the engine, fully restored to health, humming away.

'I've had her running for two hours; she's fine now.'

To demonstrate his confidence, Bill opened up the throttle, then turned her down, and our Kelvin – perhaps I should say our *new* Kelvin – first roared, and then murmured quietly.

Well, I thought, if it were done, 'twere better done well.

While all this disembowelling of the Kelvin had been going on matters were still stagnant as far as the Lister was concerned. However, Jess and I had made a determined onslaught on the last remaining problem, the stripping down of the above-water part of *Sanu*'s hull, preparatory to a complete repainting. I am afraid I had been tempted to slap on a coat of paint, like most of the fishermen do each spring, but Jess was determined that we should make a fresh start altogether. This meant buying a Calor gas torch burner and tank, and laboriously burning away the paint – not, as one might have expected, one or even two coats, but four or five.

In fact the work proved so arduous and lengthy that we were forced to call in some help from a friend of ours, Patrick, and soon life settled into quite a regular routine – Patrick would work alone all morning, and then each afternoon Jess and I would join him, and the three of us combine forces. We were very fortunate in the weather, for there was no rain, though plenty of cold winds. Gradually the bare wood of *Sanu* began to emerge, probably for the first time for twenty years ... though only briefly, for as soon as we had stripped a section, at once we quickly brushed a coat of grey primer to protect the wood. The next day we would put on one coat of undercoat, then another – until finally the whole boat, or rather all of it except one patch against the quay, was ready for the final gloss coat.

For this we mixed up a pleasing powder-blue mixture, and finally one sunny Sunday at the beginning of March, with as many members of the family as could be mustered, we set about painting the gloss coat. There was Stephen on one ladder at one end, Jess on another near him, our son-in-law Alan on another ladder in the middle, and Gill and myself on the ground doing the lower levels. It was a combined operation that had to go off at high speed, for the tide was beginning to creep in – and indeed Stephen and Alan had to finish off their parts with the bottom of their ladders in two or three feet of water ... Inevitably there was trouble – Alan's rope gave way and he fell into the water – but fortunately only up to the waist.

At last the job was finished, even to the intricate design of the name plate on either side of the bow, which Alan had touched up in black on the white background. We all went to the quay and stood looking proudly down at a graceful blue and white elegant MFV, looking quite fresh and new. Then, as a final touch, we quickly painted up our main dinghy, and labelled her proudly: *Tender to Sanu.*

At last the time arrived for the delivery to our boat of the new second engine. When Mike Peters told me it would be necessary for us to take *Sanu* over from Lelant Wharf to Hayle quay I began to feel uneasy. It was nearly six months since I had taken *Sanu* anywhere, and I was not really familiar with the intricacies of Hayle estuary. Above all, I didn't want to make a poor showing, seamanship-wise, before local experts.

'For goodness sake,' said Jess, as I lay in bed brooding, 'it's only a few hundred yards. What can possibly go wrong?'

These are famous last words, etched into my unconscious for ever.

When the afternoon came, Mike drove round to Hayle with the new engine ready to be loaded on one of the huge cranes there — while Jess and I and Stephen and Dick prepared to go over the water way.

It was a lovely sunny spring afternoon, the tide had come in fast, and it was time to go. Nervously I rushed about making sure all was well – then I went below and managed to start our diesel engine without too much fuss. On deck Dick was being rather officious about ropes and going astern before we swung her round and so on ... but I knew that his was the voice of experience and obeyed implicitly. In fact we made quite a smart getaway, steamed a hundred yards down, swung neatly round the fork in the estuary, and headed down the other stream towards the big communal quay where Mike waited with the engine.

Within a short time the 11-cwt engine had been neatly dropped on deck, Mike joined us aboard, and off we set.

'Aim for that white post, and then bring her round,' said Dick.

Feeling a growing air of confidence – even perhaps the beginnings of a pathetic secret dream that as a result of my competent handling of the boat that afternoon my status among the local fishermen would take a welcome uplift – I headed *Sanu* down by the white post. We were in rather confined waters indeed; a hundred yards away was the main quay, ahead of us a bank, to our starboard the warning posts of obstructions in the river....

'Now bring her round ... '

I hauled on the wheel. *Sanu*'s bow began to swing round, until it was heading directly for the bank on the opposite side.

'Keep bringing her round ... ' said Dick. A few moments later: 'Are you sure you're bringing her round?'

'I can't,' I ejaculated in a frantic, strained voice. 'There's something wrong.' I hauled despairingly at a suddenly immovable wheel, tugging and tugging. Suddenly it wrenched itself out of my grasp and spun madly round.

'The steering's *jammed*!'

It was, too ... Leaving us with our bow headed for a sandbank, our stern a few yards from the first of those dreaded wooden beacons, and our midships abreast of an incoming tide which would carry us very quickly upon a large quay wall.

For a moment I stood there petrified. Then Dick's calm voice sounded at my side:

'Put her into reverse. Give her a burst. Knock her out of gear.'

By these processes, miraculously it seemed, our large boat was made to stand still in mid-water. The bank, the stakes, the wall – all remained fortunately at the same distance.

Meanwhile, we tore away the floorboards and examined the chain of the wheel, which seemed to have become locked below. Hammer! Spanner! Chisel! With them Mike poked and prodded while at the wheel I frantically carried out Dick's instructions.

'Now forward a bit ... only a touch ... knock her out ... now into reverse ... a bit of throttle, not too much ... now knock her out.'

As, like a marionette, I carried out these expert instructions, a part of me managed to take in the scene. Over on the quay the men were all watching ... nearer at hand some interested spectators were gathering on the bank ... meantime in a narrow area of water, in the heart of Hayle, our boat was helplessly going round and round, liable at any moment to hit a sandbank, perhaps even a rock. Indeed it was not impossible for *Sanu* actually to sink up the estuary, a mile from the sea. What a disaster! What ignominy! How would we ever face anyone again?

'Reverse ... knock her out ... forward ...'

Relentlessly we drifted towards the wall. Then at the last minute there was a shout of triumph from Mike as he loosened the chain, and the wheel spun free.

'Righto, Cap'n – away she goes.'

Temporarily back in control if it could be called that, I sent *Sanu* forward, away from those horrid walls and stakes. Soon we came to the fork in the estuary again, and it was necessary once more to make a sweeping turn. We managed somehow to negotiate the bend safely, but as we came down to our own quay again we were faced with the need to make yet another sharp turn against the strong tide. Praying devoutly, I swung the wheel hard over. ... Prayers were not enough. There was an alarming tightening of the wheel, and all at once it became immovable.

'It's jammed again!' I cried in anguish.

This time we were even more vulnerable, broadside against a stream that would soon carry us on to a weir, with no control on the steering.

I stood there gripping the wheel forlornly. Everything was against me, we were doomed.

'Put her into reverse ... knock her out ... now forward ... knock her out ... into reverse.'

Once more quiet, knowledgeable voice came to my reason. We lumbered backwards and forwards, while Mike struggled again with the steering. Once again disaster loomed nearer and nearer, and once again at the last minute the steering was freed and we limped up against the quay ... home at last, but somewhat shaken.

After all that trouble, the new engine still had to be manoeuvred laboriously down into the aft cabin and then into the main engine-room, where Dick had cleared space for it and made a solid wooden bed. There was a lot more complicated work fitting air ducts and extending controls to the wheelhouse, but at long last, only a week or so before our winter sojourn would be ended, the second engine was finally installed and tested. It took up quite a lot of room and had cost a lot of money we could ill afford, but at least we could go to sea knowing that if anything ever did go wrong with our main engine, we were not in any danger of drifting to disaster.

And now, spring was in the air, even summertime had been brought in, during a March which had in fact begun with snowstorms and blizzards. Our winter hibernation was nearly ended. Now in the last week or so we rushed round finishing off a lot of last minute jobs, and more especially giving a last coat of gloss paint to one side of the boat which we had not been able to get at before. Our final task was to give the entire deck a final coat of red Dekaplex, hoping that, apart from the aesthetic effect, it might stop some of the odd leaks that were still bothering us.

At last one sunny afternoon we stood on the quay at Lelant looking down on what might well have been a new boat altogether. Gone were the rather drab black and faded green colours – here was a bright shining blue and white fishing vessel, as cheerful as any of the French boats. Somehow the use of the powder blue seemed to have emphasised the beauty of *Sanu*'s portly curves ... she looked, we felt proudly, quite the belle of the estuary. And eager, as we were now, to be out and about.

VIII

Around the Western Isles

For our second major voyage in *Sanu* – indeed, far and away the longest and most ambitious of all our journeys – there was a certain amount of family disagreement. Jess, tired of English weather (but blessed by a blissful ignorance of the geographical facts of life) was all for a trip to sunny Spain. Since it seemed to me that this would involve a hazardous trip across the Bay of Biscay and perhaps a total outward journey of a thousand miles, I was not enthusiastic. Besides, I had already set my nautical sights firmly in a different direction – colder and less equable, perhaps, but offering exciting prospects of grandeur and native beauty. In the end the skipper's relentless persuasiveness won the day and it was agreed that the whole of the summer school holidays should be devoted to a voyage up the west coast of England and Wales and into the romantic sounding world of the Western Isles of Scotland, or the Hebrides.

As usual I embarked on my favourite practice of gathering in a complete list of charts – this time even I was somewhat dumbfounded to find that I had to spend nearly £15 on some thirty-five separate charts (subsequently I was to be eternally grateful for such foresight, as we headed *Sanu* nervously down intricate channels between fearsome rocks and reefs). I had never been to West Scotland before, but had it firmly fixed in my mind that such misty islands as Skye and Mull and Arran were 'musts'; in addition, I had always had a yen to travel down the Caledonian Canal, which cuts Scotland in half, and also to visit the really, shorter Crinan Canal.

When finally, at eight o'clock on a late July evening, we

embarked from St Ives for Scotland, we were in the gayest of moods. All our plans had been completed satisfactorily, we were well stocked up with food and oil and water, and we were really looking forward to the complete change from a St Ives overrun by trippers, to the solitary grandeur of the Highlands. We were to be much the same contingent as had made the trip to the Channel Isles – Jess and I, Martin and Stephen and his friend, Nicky, Demelza and Genevieve, Gill and her husband, Alan, Frank and Kate Baker and their daughter, Josephine – plus one very important addition, our tiniest passenger yet: Emily, our three-month-old granddaughter of Gill and Alan. Frank and Kate and Josephine would be joining us at our first port of call, Fishguard. Meanwhile, the rest of us had a jolly parting drink at the Sloop, on the harbour front at St Ives, and it was in the cheeriest of moods that we walked along to set off. The forecast had been 3-4, which wasn't bad from our experience.

Forecast or no forecast, we had hardly left the shelter of St Ives bay when *Sanu* began lurching about violently, rolling and tossing as if in the hands of demons – a mode of travel which was to persist right through the long, long night and until dawn, breaking somewhere near the Pembrokeshire coast, heralded a welcome calming down in the weather. We were all of us sick, some several times, and it was altogether a sorry beginning to our five-week voyage. We were thoroughly glad to reach Fishguard, there to be cheerfully welcomed by our friends, unsullied by the night's experience. Truth to tell, we felt rather like staying in the protection of Fishguard harbour, but pulling ourselves resolutely together, we set off early the next morning for Holyhead, and on to the Isle of Man.

Our experience of the latter place was pleasantly surprising – we had not expected much, but in fact found the interior country (seen rather delightfully on the little railway trip from Peel to Douglas) quite lovely, and comparatively unspoiled. Peel, which was the harbour we called at – and, because of bad weather, remained in for three days – was a cosy little town, dominated by the Manx kipper. We discovered that whereas in Cornwall the tourists send their friends packets of cream, from the Isle of Man it is the Manx kipper, and we sent off several.

When at last the weather improved and we were due to leave Peel, we experienced the first of several traumatic adventures which were to colour our Scottish trip. Our berth was well up the harbour, and with several rows of Belfast fishing boats behind us the most obvious way of extricating ourselves was to turn round within the harbour. I knew there was a rather troublesome sandbank somewhere in the centre and was careful to ask a fisherman if we had enough depth to turn across it. He – thinking, I since discovered, that we had as sharp a turning point as the Belfast boats – said we would manage it easily. In good faith, therefore, I took *Sanu* hard over to port and headed down the centre of the harbour ... until suddenly the land on either side of us ceased to move by, and we realised we had run aground. What's more (and much worse) aground on a falling tide.

For five or ten minutes we ran both engines flat out, reversing and then changing forward, then back to reverse again – all without avail. Then much to our relief, there were some reassuring calls from among the Belfast men, and to our great relief we saw two of their hefty 60-foot trawlers getting up steam and beginning to move out. Apparently it was a fairly common occurrence for boats to get caught on this sandbank, including the fishermen themselves, so they understood the predicament only too well. In no time at all they had manoeuvred near enough to take our ropes and with several sharp tugs – it was not by any means all that easy, with the tide falling rapidly – managed to haul us free.

Our troubles, however, were not over. After this rather shattering experience, we put in to the outer end of the quay, partly to thank our rescuers, partly to fill up with water. As we came in, fortunately very slowly indeed, I had a strange impression that when I put the boat into reverse, nothing really happened. However, we had got our ropes ashore by then and tied up, so I said nothing until I had been over to thank the fishermen. When I came back, Stephen was shaking his head dolefully.

'The propeller wasn't going round when you reversed.'

We stood staring unhappily into the green water, trying not to credit this latest prospect of disaster. What could have happened?

At that very moment a couple more Belfast fishermen stepped aboard with friendly grins. I can't possibly reproduce the Belfast brogue, except to say that to us southerners it was almost incomprehensible. However, I gathered that they were saying they had heard we might be having a bit of engine trouble, could they help?

'Well,' I said dubiously, 'our reverse seems a bit dicey.'

It was more than that, as they speedily proved – it had packed up. For the very simple reason – our shaft that runs from the engine to the propeller is in two parts, joined by a coupling, and the rear section had slipped out of the coupling.

On my own such an occurrence would have seemed the direst disaster, since it posed a problem new to me and I really had no idea what had to be done to repair matters. Not so our two Belfast friends – they were very familiar with such an occurrence from their own boats, and they knew exactly what had to be done.

It was a process of laborious work with mallet and crowbar and spanners that took about four or five hours, but at the end of it, miraculously, our shafts were joined again – and this time, we had a shrewd idea, more strongly than ever before. During the whole time Stephen and I had watched with close interest, and we had the added comfort that, if the same thing happened some other time in the future, we now knew exactly what to do.

We insisted on paying the fishermen something for their troubles, but we knew that this wasn't important – what was very touching to us was the knowledge that these men just naturally came to our aid out of good fellowship. This was a warming trait we also found among the Scottish fishermen – ever ready to lend a hand, to give advice. This is probably a characteristic of fishermen everywhere, but nowhere have we found it more readily evident than during our Scottish trip.

The next day the weather really cleared and we made a good trip up to Stranraer and then on up the Firth of Clyde past

Arran and up Loch Fynne to the port of Tarbert. This was probably the finest day of all our trip, the sun blazing down, the sea as calm as the proverbial millpond – and all around us such fascinating sights as Ailsa Craig, rising up in stark granite splendour in the middle of nowhere, and then the wild grandeur of Arran and its Holy Isle. There was literally not a tremor on the still waters, and the entire crew displayed themselves in bikinis and shorts and busily took photographs. The sort of day, indeed, that makes cruising worth while. And then when we finally reached Tarbert, that wonderfully sheltered harbour, we were absolutely delighted, for it is a charming centre, with a beautiful setting – indeed we liked it so much that we stayed on there an extra day in order to help Martin celebrate his twenty-first birthday.

After Tarbert, the Crinan Canal. This is a much smaller and narrower canal than the Caledonian, but I had made sure that our dimensions would just fit in with its maximum requirements of 88ft long, 22 ft beam and 9 ft 6 in draft. All the same its winding and torturous passage from Ardrishaig Basin, in the south, to Crinan at the north end, provided me, as helmsman, with many headaches. Sometimes, indeed, we could have reached out and touched the foliage growing on either bank – what we could have done if we met another large boat like ourselves, goodness only knows (I discovered later that the lock-keepers pass on information of every craft coming and going, so that if necessary one can be held back for the arrival of another).

Although only nine miles long the canal was divided by fifteen locks, mostly the old-fashioned sort where our crew had to lend a hand in winding and unwinding the gates – but, just as I had imagined, it made a pleasant change. Sometimes the setting of the canal was quite breathtaking, winding among huge banks of trees, or opening out upon a picture-book panorama of flat land and distant mountains. In addition to the locks every now and then we came round a bend to encounter a swing bridge, whose operator had to be summoned by an urgent blast on our hooter – sometimes opening his bridge only at the very last moment!

Somehow we managed to survive what to me was quite a tricky passage, and ended up in Crinan Basin, along with a dozen or so other craft of various shapes and sizes. Here we had our first exciting view of Hebridean waters, and we felt we were really on our way.

After a call the next day for replenishments at Oban we made our way up Loch Linnhe and Loch Lorne, past the Corran Narrows and Fort William, and came to our second and much larger canal – the Caledonian. Long before we came to the entry port of Corpach we had sensed a formidable change in our surroundings. We were now among *real* mountains – to one side at the rear the towering peaks of Mull, then the equally striking peaks of Morvern – and now at last, stretching away into the very heavens, the huge mountains behind Fort William, rising in the end to Ben Nevis, highest in the British Isles. From the flat sea-loch at Corpach it made a truly impressive sight; and later that evening, after we had made a rather laborious climb through the 'staircase' of eight locks at Banavie, Frank and Kate and Jess and I strolled along the quiet leafy banks of the canal and marvelled at the lovely setting.

In fact, as we progressed farther and farther along the sixty-mile long canal (which links the North Sea and the Atlantic Ocean, and provides a safe sheltered passage, as against the rough outer route *via* Cape Wrath and the Minch) we were all agreed that the Caledonian truly justified all the glowing remarks we had heard about its beauty and peacefulness. Possibly what contributed to this was the fact that at three points the canal opens out into a lovely 'inland sea' – Loch Lochy, Loch Oich and Loch Ness: on the other hand I have clear memories of winding canal banks, man-made, often hewn out of rocky countryside, which could rival nature in their beauty.

We had soon reached the highest point at Laggan Locks, and then gradually began descending, notably at Fort Augustus, where there was another 'staircase', this time of five descending locks. Here we made our long-awaited entry into the famous Loch Ness, which is itself about 25 miles long. We had the rather uncanny experience of travelling up the loch on an eerie misty afternoon, so that at any moment we expecting to see 'the monster'. However, the next day the mist was gone, and it was so sunny and warm that Frank fulfilled his ambition to have a swim in the Ness – the rest of us lacked his courage, and went instead for a long country walk. We had anchored the boat by Temple Pier, opposite Urquhart Castle, and this was the farthest point of our journey east.

Here, Frank and Martin had to take their leave, catching a taxi into Inverness to meet the night train bound for London and work. After waving them goodbye we pulled up our anchor and set off back to Fort Augustus, and then on the next day to Banavie and, the following morning, out of the canal altogether.

During this, our first fortnight of the cruise, we had been blessed with excellent weather, every day sunny and blue – so much so that I was constantly taunting Jess, who had dolefully repeated the prognostications of her sister, Marjorie, that it was always raining in Scotland. Now the weather showed signs of flagging, but we did not particularly notice it at the time for we had a new interest – finding Llewellyn. Llewellyn was Kate Baker's son, who had recently married and taken a share in a fishing boat in Scotland, and was reputed to be travelling in it to Mull. Even in the canal we had often strained our eyes trying to identify Llew's craft, which Kate rather vaguely defined as 'about twenty-five feet, a converted lifeboat, with a wheel-house'. Now, as we proceeded back down Lochs Linnhe and Lorne we kept a hopeful eye out, but with no luck.

Towards the end of that day it began raining in that earnest, continual way which we came regretfully to associate with Scotland, and we were very glad to reach our haven for the night, Loch Aline. The entry was a tricky one over a sand bar, but once inside there was plenty of room to anchor. Indeed, in the starboard corner there were already three or four yachts, and I dutifully brought *Sanu* up alongside them, and we put over the anchor while I reversed … or rather, tried to reverse. Suddenly there was an almighty clattering noise, and I hastily put the engine into neutral, while like a bullet Stephen shot below. When he came back, his face was grim.

'It's the coupling – it's slipped again.'

This was bad enough news – in addition, already, we could see that our anchor was not holding firm, and we were dragging, and gradually drifting across the loch. There was nothing for it but to pull up the anchor and try anchoring again. This we did; twenty minutes later we were dragging again. Finally, on the third attempt, the anchor seemed to hold, and, exhausted, we went down to supper – aware only too well that the larger problem of the shaft awaited our attention.

That night Stephen, Nicky and Alan spent several hours laboriously fitting the coupling back into place ... only to find to their chagrin that as soon as we tested the reverse in the morning it slipped out again. There was nothing for it but to try to get the boat out of what suddenly seemed a lonely and god-forsaken loch to somewhere comparatively civilised, where mechanical assistance could be found. Since we could not use the main engine this meant trusting entirely to the small wing engine. If we had been faced with the open sea I would have had my doubts, but since it was only ten miles up the Sound of Mull to Tobermory, the main town of the island, I felt we ought to be able to manage.

In fact, our progress was excruciatingly slow, hardly three knots compared to our usual eight – but after three worried hours we finally brought the boat into Tobermory's sheltered harbour and anchored opposite the pier. At once I had the dinghy over the side and rushed ashore to try to find an engineer. The only possible man was busy the rest of that day but he promised to come out at nine o'clock the next morning, and we had to be satisfied with that.

Meantime, seeing posters about advertising the annual cattle show at Salen, farther up the coast, we all piled into one of the MacBrayne's coaches and made a very hazardous and torturous journey whizzing up and down narrow cliff roads. It was interesting to see gathered into one large field what was obviously a very thorough cross-section of the population of Mull (which in all I believe is under 3,000); even more fascinating to see a fine selection of Highland cattle, with their strange beatnik hair style. We thoroughly enjoyed the day out and returned full of confidence that in the morning things would soon be put right, and we would be on our way.

In fact, we had an excellent young engineer to attend to the shaft, and he made a fine job of fixing it, so that we were able to start off on the next leg of our journey towards Skye. Unfortunately, had we but known it, our troubles – notably our anchoring troubles, which henceforth were to dominate our Scottish voyaging – were only just beginning. When we took up anchor and set off from Tobermory the weather seemed very sheltered, but no sooner had we shown our nose outside than conditions changed markedly. Usually I always get a weather forecast before moving, but this was midday, and I thought, well, anyway, we can hear the two o'clock forecast.

By the time we heard the two o'clock forecast, with its alarming sudden warning of Force 8, possibly gale, for the Hebrides, we had almost reached Ardnamurchan Point ... where faced not only by an ugly and rising sea but the added hazard of a real Scottish mist, for the first time in my life I turned my boat back. After all, we were on holiday, boating for pleasure, and none of us fancied three or four hours in a Hebridean gale.

I can hardly doubt that this was a correct decision (in fact the gale conditions persisted for the next three days and brought other ships scuttling into Tobermory) and yet when I think of the consequences ... First, we came back into Tobermory and dropped our anchor rather nearer into shore. An hour or two later, looking round uneasily, I wondered if we were not dragging a little, but decided to leave it for the time being. After another hour it became pretty evident ... around eight o'clock in the evening I could put off the evil moment no longer, for we were perilously near the harbour shore.

'Stephen! Alan! Nicky! Afraid we'll have to get the anchor up, we're dragging badly.'

Owing to the fact that the teeth on our winch are rather badly worn, winding up the anchor chain on *Sanu* is quite a performance, as one person has to stand on the incoming

chain in order to obtain a real grip. However, we duly wound
in the anchor and I put the engine into gear and headed *Sanu*
away from the shore. Now a nightmarish experience began. In
the first place, because of the gale quite a lot of boats had
accumulated in Tobermory harbour – as I now looked about
me they seemed to be dotted about everywhere.

Suddenly I began to realise that finding a safe anchorage was
not going to be too easy, with such a large boat as ours. One of
the difficulties at Tobermory is that the harbour is
exceptionally deep, right up to the shore, so that one had to
anchor fairly close in. Now, as time after time I took *Sanu* out
into the centre and then headed cautiously close in, I found it
impossible to find a space large enough to enable us to safely
drop anchor and be sure of not swinging back on to one of the
dozens of anchored boats.

At first it seemed fairly amusing, but as time went on and
dusk began to threaten our smiles faded. Once, in desperation,
we went right over to the heavily-wooded far shore and
dropped our anchor in a spot perilously close to the rocky
beach. It required only about a quarter of an hour's wait to
decide hurriedly that this was no place to be, and once again
we had wearily to pull up the chain.

By now it really was dusk, and suddenly things became very
unfunny, and quite worrying. For here I was at the wheel of
what in a fairly confined space was something of a dangerous
monster. A boat like *Sanu*, 60 ft long and 18 ft beam, is not
exactly easy to manoeuvre at the best of times. Now, as I
weaved endlessly between rows of anchored yachts, each time I
was forced to slow down, naturally the steerage became more
difficult. Added to that the canopy of dusk shrouding the scene
meant that everything was twice as difficult. No wonder that
one scared yachtswoman, leaning out of her 2-footer,
screamed: 'Careful, you'll kill us all!'

In fact we didn't really go dangerously close to anyone, but
for the helmsman it was a terrible tension; while always there
was the haunting knowledge that even if we dropped anchor,
we might well drag again (last time when the anchor came up it
was covered entirely by thick wads of bright green seaweed, no

doubt the cause of its not gripping). In the end, by now quite emotionally exhausted, I felt we could not face the prospect of being at the mercy of our wayward anchor in total darkness. There was one deep water quay at Tobermory (in fact because of the gale it was already occupied by a sheltering cruise steamer). Fortunately there was also a smaller stone quay used by local boats, which dried out. This was occupied by one of the Clyde 'puffer' boats, small cargo boats that deliver to the islands – but at least the tide was in. Perhaps we could manage to get in and tie up alongside?

And so, shrouded in darkness but guided by the lights of the quay I brought *Sanu* carefully up alongside the SS *Halcyon* ... and thankfully we tied our ropes to her solid iron samsonpost and then hurriedly put down our port leg while we had the chance (when I looked at the echo sounder, we had about one foot of water under us, and the tide was already turning).

'Well,' we thought thankfully, 'safe at last.'

So we were, but there was still a price to pay. Although we put our half a dozen rubber tyres as fenders before going to bed it had not occurred to us that such a large boat – she must have been half as long again as us, and much broader – might actually be considerably shallower than *Sanu*. In fact, whereas we drew seven and a half feet, *Halcyon* only drew between five and six feet. As a result, when we were afloat, her wide iron rib, or buffer, was *above* our wooden fender rail – but when we went aground, she continued to drop and drop *and* drop, and eventually her massive fender just broke off a section of ours. It was nothing vitally damaging, but annoying and inconvenient, as well as looking very untidy.

However, during the two enforced gale-bound days we now spent at the quay we soon overcame our annoyance and became friendly with the cheery crew of the *Halcyon* – a boat, we learned, that had been playing the islands' run for more than fifty years, under the same captain. He was stern, and made in the old-fashioned mould – and every Sunday was to be seen soberly dressed carrying his Bible and heading for the kirk – but he knew every inch of the Hebridean coast, and his young crew had complete faith in him. From what we could make out there was good money in this pleasantly independent form of trading and they were all sad that in another year the boat was due for the scrapyard.

At last the weather improved. Now I was plagued by the fear that during neap tides our boat would never get off the bottom at the quay ... and in the end, indeed, it was only by arising at 4 a.m. and having the engines running at exactly the moment of high tide that we managed to edge *Sanu* out into deeper water, and be on our way ... very glad, I must say, to leave Tobermory, picturesque and sheltered though it may be.

This time we were heading round Ardnamurchan and northwards, past Mallaig, and into the Sound of Sleat. *En route* we passed, to port, the formidable mountainous islands of Eigg and Rhum, and the smaller one of Muick. It was a pleasant enough journey (which we could imagine would have been hell in a Force 8 gale) and by midday we had actually reached our fifty-mile-away objective, the renowned and beautiful Loch Duich. I had read so much about this spot, and seen such lovely photographs of its water-surrounded castle, that I was afraid of being disappointed. But in fact it really was most beautiful, especially at the far end of the loch, where the horizon was dominated by mountains known as the Five Sisters.

Once again, though, our peace of mind was plagued by anchor trouble; our first anchoring, in what was supposed to be the most sheltered spot, Totaig Bay, lasted five hours, then we began dragging badly. We hauled in, went into the bay again, and this time dropped not only our CQR anchor on the chain, but also put our huge old fisherman, on a nylon rope. All to no avail; half an hour later we were dragging badly towards a small rocky islet. Now when we pulled in the two anchors, the chain and rope became entangled, and we were all swearing and exhausted again when finally I headed *Sanu* away down to the very end of the loch, where we managed to find a really sheltered and peaceful anchorage for the night.

The next morning we were off again, bound at last for the romantic island of Skye itself, the northernmost objective of our trip. Now the weather really had deteriorated, and we were plagued by what we came to recognise as typical Scottish mists, which made navigation more difficult than usual. I was heartily relieved when we reached Ramsay Sound, and headed towards Portree, the 'capital' of Skye. This was a town and setting not unlike Tobermory, but more highly geared to the tourist industry. However, we were so relieved to be somewhere where we did not have to anchor, being allowed to berth alongside the pier, that we forgave Portree its concessions to tripperdom, and enjoyed two relaxed days exploring the local sights.

By now weather delays had made us very much behind on our itinerary, so at the first reasonable forecast we set off on the last leg of our northern-bound voyage – from Portree up the north-east coast of Skye, and round Eileen Troddday Island, and then down the north-west coast. Scenically it was a magnificent trip, the vast towering cliffs of Skye being quite breathtaking seen from seawards ... but weather conditions altered for the worse after we had rounded Trodday, and for the remaining twenty-five miles, across Vatternish Point and round Dunvegan, we had a big sea coming right across us that was thoroughly uncomfortable.

Loch Dunvegan, I felt sure, would make up for all that. There was a lovely sheltered anchorage below the famous castle – the only inhabited castle in west Scotland, home then of Dame Flora Macleod, and gathering place once a year for Macleods from all over the world. Yes, it was all there, and we came round the last point into sheltered waters and dropped our anchor, and then our other anchor – and, lo and behold, they seemed to be holding, yes, they really were holding. That night, to celebrate this unusual event, we went ashore in the two dinghies, and the older ones among us enjoyed an unexpectedly cheerful evening in the comfortable Dunvegan Hotel. Chugging back in the moonlight was a very romantic experience, and I dismissed from my mind the tiny suspicion that maybe the anchor light on *Sanu* seemed rather farther away than when we had set out.

At least we did have a good night's sleep. But by midday the next day it became only too sadly evident that our old trouble was back, the anchor was dragging – and indeed *Sanu* was getting perilously near to a group of tiny rocky islets that surround the base of Dunvegan Castle.

'Nothing for it,' I groaned. 'Let's start the engine.'

Usually our Kelvin starts on a half swing. Today was going to be different. It would not start on a half swing, nor a whole swing, nor a dozen such swings. Exhausted I stepped aside and Alan took over. Soon the sweat was pouring down his brow, and still the engine would not catch. Becoming uneasy I ran upstairs and took one look. We were indeed very, very close to the rocks. Beside me Stephen looked agitated.

'Start the Lister, Dad – quick!'

I hesitated.

'But that's only a small engine! Will it get us out of here?'

It soon became evident that the question was an academic one: if the Lister wouldn't get us out, then we would go on the rocks. Quickly we started up our new smaller engine – and for the umpteenth time I thanked my lucky stars that we had put in a second engine. Then we went up deck again and began winding in our two anchors.

Now began what I suppose, in retrospect, was the most excruciating and dangerous experience of the whole trip. For when the anchor finally came up and I put the Lister on to full power and into forward gear, the wind and tide had whipped up so strongly (as seems invariable in our adventures, the weatherman chose this moment to inflict us with what turned out to be the beginning of a real gale, strong even in that supposedly sheltered part) that I just could not bring *Sanu*'s bow round enough to clear the line of the rocky shore ahead of us.

I kept going forward until the last possible moment, and then had hurriedly to put her into reverse. But here again, there was a snag – some way behind us lay the rock-infested shore at the base of the castle. Could we manage to come round in reverse enough to clear that and emerge safely, if rearwards, into the fairway? No, it soon became evident, we could not.

And so the ridiculous process began, forwards up to one shore, backwards to the opposite shore – without gaining anything, and in fact, very subtly losing some ground so that all the time we were being pushed sideways towards a rocky islet in the centre of the bay.

By now we were all becoming thoroughly alarmed – even, understandably, a little hysterical. To come all these hundreds of miles up to and around the wild Hebrides and to aground in a sheltered loch! It was ridiculous. And yet there was no doubt it was going to happen if we did not manage some kind of miracle. We tried everything. At one stage Nicky bravely got into the white motor dinghy with the forlorn idea of tugging the bows round – but by now the waves were so nasty that he was almost swamped and had to swarm back up the rope. After that the three boys stayed down in the engine room trying forlornly to start our recalcitrant main engine.

For myself, I was becoming truly desperate. 'Please, *please* come round,' I begged *Sanu*'s lumpy bows – but always they half came round and then stuck. It became evident that the forward-reverse procedure could not go on much longer, or we would be thrown on to the middle island. In desperation I considered my one remaining alternative – to go farther in, and try to round the islet from the inside.

According to the chart this inner area was strewn with rocks. I had no idea of the depths; it would an absolute gamble. On the other hand, it would mean turning *Sanu*'s bow to starboard instead of port, and with our wing engine fixed on the port side this would give us a much stronger steerage. Maybe, maybe we could manage? Well, we would have to!

Praying silently, I headed *Sanu* between one rocky shore and the rocky islet, while the rest of my crew who were on deck looked at me in amazement. There wasn't time for any explanations, all we could do was to hold on, while I kept the wheel hard over ... all the time expecting any moment to hear the horrid crunch of rock driving into *Sanu*'s hull.

It seemed to last an eternity, but I suppose took about three or four minutes – then, miraculously, we had rounded the islet and were safely back in the fairway, heading away from danger, and towards a distant wharf, used by cargo boats, but which now, at all costs, was going to be our home. A few minutes later we were safely tied up there, and trying to unwind our tensed limbs from what was our narrowest ever squeak.

After such an experience we might surely have felt entitled to some relaxation, but the sea is not like that. The wind, which had been freshening, quickly assumed gale proportions, so that even inside the loch we were considerably exposed. The pier at which we were moored was a wooden one, and not over-strong, and now it creaked and groaned. More worryingly, it was the night of an exceptionally high tide, and soon we found to our alarm that *Sanu* appeared to be rising so high that she would surely be on the pier itself. This fate was averted, but our fenders were rendered pretty useless, and the wooden piles of the pier rubbed uncomfortably against our side all night.

On the other hand the sudden gale brought us some good fortune – late that evening a fishing boat came alongside, its crew looking bleary-eyed from crossing the Minch in what they swore was a Force 9. Their boat was bound for Mallaig with a big catch of lobsters, so if they put in for shelter, it must have been bad. They were just as friendly as the Belfast men had been made us take some lobsters as a gift – and later in the evening, on learning of our mechanical trouble, their engineer came across and spent an hour taking ours to pieces and tracing the fault. By then Jess and I had crept miserably to bed, leaving Stephen and Alan to cope, but as the engine-room is beneath our cabin we heard snatches of conversation, and gathered hopefully that some repair was being executed. Sure enough, after a fair while, there was the sudden healthy throb of the Kelvin roaring into life again.

Just as at the beginning of our trip the weather had been kind to us, now it was perverse and tormenting. After a slightly better forecast we set out on the long trip around the point of Dunvegan – by then we were somewhat committed and grimly ploughed our way through what must have been Force 6-7 until the welcome sight of the small island of Canna offered us a chance to take shelter.

Originally Canna had been on our list, then in the effort to make up lost time I had cut it out – now, as we nosed up to the tiny quay in complete shelter from the elements raging outside, I was heartily glad of our choice. Of all the places we visited, in many ways Canna was most intriguing: a small narrow island on which some twenty people live, mostly in crofts, and mostly working for one man, the laird. Despite the tiny population, it was competitively served by two churches – a Roman Catholic one at one end, and a tiny Presbyterian one on the opposite hill. There was no shop, only a small post office – if you wanted provisions you ordered them from Mallaig on the four-times-a-week steamer – and paid about 2s in the £1 carriage.

We talked to one or two inhabitants and found them quite content – and indeed why not, in this age of strain and rush? Everything on Canna seemed pleasantly uncomplicated, and orderly – crops to be got in, animals to be tended, vegetables to be grown in the back garden. The island itself had a strange quiet beauty – and for a more grand landscape there was always the vast tips of Rhum just across the water. We liked Canna very much, and were sorry to leave.

Our next journey took us down past Coll and then round the strange flat-topped Treshnish Isles, and Staffa with its weird Fingal's Cave – and into Lock Lathaich, on the Ross of Mull. According to the Clyde Sailing Club's Guide Book this offered the perfect sheltered anchorage, but for once in a way they must have erred a little, for we found it dreadfully exposed to the prevailing conditions.

And once again – I don't want to become a bore but it happened! – we were in serious trouble over anchoring. First the anchor refused to hold at all, though we put out five times the length of chain – so we wound it up again and had another try, this time putting out the old fisherman as well. This time we seemed to be well and truly held, in the lee of a small island, so Alan and Nick and Kate hurriedly got into a dinghy and rowed ashore to a small pier, to go into Bunessan for some provisions. I felt uneasy at thus being left with only Stephen and Jess to help if anything went wrong.

Sure enough, after twenty minutes we began dragging badly. And of course when we tried to bring in the anchors they once again got entangled. By this time I had both engines going and was in ample control of the boat, but we simply weren't in a position to do anything about dropping anchors until we had got them untangled, and on our own couldn't cope.

At this moment Kate and Nick and Alan were to be seen on the pier, getting into the dingy, and we waited ... and waited until at last it dawned on us that although they were trying desperately to row out, the pressure of wind and waves coming straight on to the shore made it impossible. In fact, they were helpless, tied to the shore! Well, this offered a clue to our own destination: fortunately it was near high tide, and from the chart I estimated that it was just about safe to go alongside the pier. Originally the idea was to pick up the others, but once we were there and found we did float at high tide, we jumped for joy – and put out our leg, and furiously tied up. Safe again from the hazards of anchoring.

After a fascinating visit to Iona, nearby, whose picturesque setting reminded us very much of Cornwall, we were off again on the longest day voyage of the trip, some ninety-five miles past Colonsay and Oronsay and through the Sound of Islay and down the long Mull of Kintyre. We had all heard forbidding tales of this dreaded point, but on this particular day the sea was smooth and unruffled, and we had our second sunniest day of the whole voyage – a glorious trip, right round and into the sheltered loch of Campbeltown. There we were back among fishing boats again, and quite a busy little town, and we were able to celebrate our second birthday, this time Demelza's fourteenth, with a dinner at the Royal Hotel. The next morning we were up early and off to Peel on yet another long leg.

At last we felt definitely on the way home, and were glad enough, after our hectic and varied five weeks. There was a momentary and rather ludicrous hold-up when, as we left Peel, our rudder jammed, and we had to manoeuvre ourselves cumbersomely back to the quay in order to fix it – then we were off on another sunny voyage down to Holyhead. Here we were droppping off Kate and Josephine, so instead of anchoring I decided to take *Sanu* into the commercial part of the port, where there is one public quay which the harbour master had told me was available 'first come, first served'. We found a berth all right, but were immediately assailed by a bevy of officials who warned us of the dire consequences likely to result – our ropes would be parted by the vast wash from the mail steamers, not to mention eight cargo boats coming by in the middle of the night. We were somewhat alarmed and put out extra ropes, but in fact it was all poppycock and we were hardly disturbed at all. And we were very glad we had gone to that quay, for it was near to the railway station where, soon after midnight, we all gave a lively send off to Kate and Josephine on their journey through the night to Cardiff.

Our reason for dropping them off at Holyhead instead of Fishguard was that I had decided to make the trip from Holyhead to St Ives in one hop. This meant leaving Holyhead in darkness at the unholy hour of 4 a.m. – in order, according to my thrice-checked calculations, to reach St Ives the next morning about 6 am, and so catch the early morning tide and not have to anchor for hours outside.

Well, we managed our getaway, and soon the winking light of South Stack was behind us, and we had a trouble-free run down past Bardsey Island and nearly to the Smalls – then our luck changed. Waves got bigger and bigger, the wind blew harder, and the remaining ninety miles, through a long, long night, were about as uncomfortable as had been our very first trip outward. Only by now we were such acclimatized sailors that fortunately no one was sick. We took it in shifts to steer, three hours on and six hours off.

My turn was the last one, from three in the morning, and soon after coming on I was delighted to see the beam of Pendeen lighthouse ahead. My pleasure faded somewhat as (a) we failed to find Godrevy light and (b) a thick sleeting rain began blowing in our faces, and clouding the visibility. As a result, until dawn, we were forced to slow down, and content ourselves with two or three nervous trips up and down the coast by Pendeen.

At last, however, there was a glimmer of light and soon we identified Zennor Head, and were able to head back to Clodgy Point and the Island. At a few minutes past six o'clock we came zooming into the bay, both engines going full blast in case we missed the tide, and soon after we had nosed up to the quay at St Ives and were tying up – home at last after a trip which, we calculated, had covered more than 1,500 miles. We were all exhausted and in need of a bath, but we also felt a real pride in the achievement.

The next day we took *Sanu* over to Hayle and berthed her safely for the winter. And the day after that – we began thinking about our next season!

IX

A Local Industry

Painting is now so popular in Cornwall as to be almost a local industry in itself. Certainly, with the possible exception of London, there can be nowhere else in the British Isles where so many professional artists live and work. St Ives, Newlyn, Mousehole, Lamorna Cove, the Lizard, Falmouth, Fowey, Mevagissey, Polperro, Looe, Tintagel, Boscastle, Port Isaac, Padstow, Wadebridge – in almost every corner of the county, working in converted fish cellars, in wide-windowed lofts, in old-fashioned wooden studios and in bright new concrete ones built to specification, artists of varied outlooks and techniques have not only made homes but in many cases reputations. The result has been the creation of something quite unique in British life, usually more associated with the Mediterranean – genuine cosmopolitan and colourful art colonies, buzzing with creative life.

Like most other visitors the artists have always been immediately impressed by their first contact with Cornwall, its light and scenery, its atmosphere and old traditions. The famous nineteenth-century engraver Thomas Rowlandson once made a journey round the coast out of which he produced several scores of vivid black and white etchings of the craggy cliffs, wild moorland and huddled fishing ports.

Three years after the Duke of Wellington had won the Battle of Waterloo, that great landscape painter, J.M.W. Turner, a revolutionary in the art movement of his time, visited St Ives and was absolutely enchanted by the light and conditions. Near the end of the nineteenth century two more famous painters, Whistler and Sickert, both spent a winter in St Ives with extremely productive results.

It was about this time that Cornish art colony life began with the arrival in neighbouring Newlyn of Walter Langley, T.C. Gotch, Frank Bramley, Stanhope Forbes and other young painters filled with the then startling new ideas of painting all their pictures direct from Nature. Many of these painters had been influenced by the realist outlook of some of the French painters such as Millet, Courbet and Bastien-Lepage; some, like Stanhope Forbes, has already experimented with painting members of a primitive peasant community in Brittany.

Cornwall has many historical and geographical similarities with Brittany, as well as the same warm climate, and it is easy to imagine how the young painters travelled eagerly down to this new world of picturesque fishing villages, unspoiled by industrialism, where they could find not only cheap living but plenty of colourful models among the fishing community and all the vivid background they could possibly require for their open air paintings.

In an article in the *Cornish Magazine* in 1898 Stanhope Forbes, who came to be regarded as the father of the Newlyn Movement, has left us a charming picture of those early days of the 1880's when artists first descended in large numbers on the simple fishing folk:

> These were the days of unflinching realism, of the cult of Bastien-Lepage. It was part of our artistic creed to paint our pictures direct from Nature, and not merely to rely upon sketches and studies which we could afterwards amplify in the comfort of a studio. Artists are common enough objects by the seaside; but it was scarcely so usual to see the painter not merely engaged upon a small sketch or panel, but with a large canvas securely fastened to some convenient boulder, absorbed in the very work with which he hoped to win fame in the ensuing spring; perhaps even the model posing in full view of the entire populace, the portrait being executed with a publicity calculated to unnerve even our practised brother of the pavement.

These singular goings on of the newcomers at first

provoked much comment from the inhabitants, but by degrees they grew familiar with such strange doings, and scarce heeded the work which progressed before their eyes. Even the small folk grew tired of gazing, and at that dread moment when the school doors opened and let loose upon their chosen victims the arch tormentors of our race, a few moments of misery would ensue, and the harassed painter, with a sigh of relief, would find himself alone, once more free to continue his labours undisturbed.

Nothing, too, could exceed the good nature with which the local folk came to regard behaviour which might well have been thought intrusive ... I scarcely ever remember asking permission to set up my easel without it being freely accorded.

Stanhope Forbes was writing about Newlyn where he and his fellow 'revolutionaries' set out to produce a series of huge canvases of life in a fishing village; portraits of the fishermen in their blue jerseys and white duck frocks and sea-going boots, their wives in black shawls and aprons, the children playing in the cobbled streets – and also quite melodramatic scenes, such as a mourning feast, or a wedding breakfast, or the crew of the lifeboat setting out on a mercy mission.

At that time this kind of painting was much frowned upon by the critics in this country, and when the Newlyn School, as the early group was known, began to show at the Royal Academy their work was violently attacked as 'immoral'. However the critics changed their minds, as is so often the case, and there was soon a wide demand for the story-telling interiors of Stanhope Forbes, the enormous exterior canvases of Norman Garstin (often painted under terrible outside weather conditions, as in the case of his famous 'The Rain it Raineth Every Day'), and the work of a wide number of artists such as Gotch, Langley, Edwin Harris, Bramley, Fred Hall, Sherwood Hunter, Chevalier Taylor, and Ralph Todd.

Stanhope Forbes and his wife Elizabeth, also well-known as a painter, opened a busy and successful art school, and soon the public interest in the activities at Newlyn led to the opening of the Newlyn Art Gallery, financed by the generosity of a London newspaper proprietor, J.Passmore Edwards. Here were hung many paintings which have since been acquired by the Tate and other galleries all over the world. Although the activities of the Newlyn School were to dwindle for a time the present day Newlyn-Orion gallery, under the enthusiastic guidance of John Halkes, is more active and enterprising than for a long time.

As Stanhope Forbes and his friends were settling in Newlyn, so other painters were being attracted to St Ives, on the other coast, where, among other things, the light was even more translucently clear. In time many of the Newlyn painters lent their support to the developments at St Ives, which gradually came to replace Newlyn as the hub of artistic activities, with the settling in the towns of such eminent painters as Julius Olsson, Algernon Talmage, T.Millie Dow, Louis Grier, Lowell Dyer, Anders Zorn, Noble Barlow and Alfred East.

At that time, of course, St Ives was still principally a busy fishing port, and the increasing activities of the painters were viewed with some suspicion. There are many stories related which illustrate this antagonism, much of which was probably associated with the dogmatic religious attitudes of the local people of those days. Perhaps the general attitude was best summed up by a story which Algernon Talmage was fond of telling, of how a fish-cart was being driven up Skidden Hill and the horse jibbed. After exhausting an extensive vocabulary of abuse the driver, walking in the road, exclaimed, as if with his last breath, 'You – you bloody *artist!*'

Over the years St Ives has not only nurtured the large and strongly traditional St Ives Society of Artists but also provided the setting for the avant garde Penwith Society of Artists who, with substantial backing from the Arts Council, have established a large gallery as well as several workshops and artist's studios in Back Road West, in the old quarters of St Ives.

Since those early days, of course, the art colonies of Cornwall have spread enormously, though still centred mainly in the western tip, around Newlyn and St Ives. As the movement has enlarged, so the aims of the artists have widened and developed enormously, in parallel to the movements in the world of art generally. In the past few decades, for instance, what might have seemed once daring ideas of the Stanhope Forbes group have been far outstripped by modern movements such as surrealism, abstract art and so forth – with numerous distinguished practitioners, such as Ben Nicholson, Barbara Hepworth, Peter Lanyon, Patrick Heron, Gabo, Bryan Wynter. Today the Penwith Gallery at St Ives, and the Newlyn Orion Gallery at Newlyn, are two of the most important art galleries in Britain, and house a continuous stream of outstanding exhibitions.

Perhaps even more interesting than the physical existence of the art colonies has been the increasingly articulate explanation, by the artists themselves, of just what has drawn them to Cornwall, rather than any other part of Britain. The explanation is a mixture of material and mystical, factual and fantastical, all equally important. The climate, the brilliant light, the Mediterranean blue of the seas, the fascinating formations of rocks and cliffs, hills and valleys, sand and pebble stones – these are some of the more obvious attractions.

So, too, the comparative freedom and easiness of life in a small but surprisingly cosmopolitan town such as St Ives or Polperro, as compared to most English provincial towns; the congenial atmosphere of working and living among large groups of fellow artists; the facilities of numerous art galleries and showrooms, dozens of art societies and clubs; and last but by no means least a sympathetic local population and press, conditioned by several decades of growing up alongside art colonies, so that what might seem an oddity if dumped in some other part of Britain has come to be taken for granted in Cornwall.

Yes, *but* ... surely there is something else? Something less easily explained and put into words, yet with perhaps just as strong an influence on artists as the magnetic pull granite often exerts on ship's compasses? There is, indeed, and how better to attempt to capture this unkown quantity than by asking the artists themselves. Jack Pender, a native of Mousehole and a leading member of the Penwith and Newlyn Society of Artists:

> Oh, yes, there's a spiritual something here. I have met different people who have reacted to it in different ways: those who come for a week and have stayed years, and those who couldn't stand it and cleared out quickly. Through the war, art training and later teaching, I was out of Cornwall for twenty years ... this thing gradually grew on me, I experienced it when I came home on leave or holiday ... it became an obsession. I *had* to get back. Even when out of Cornwall I found myself painting pictures of Cornwall, subjects I had remembered. The whole thing became very intense. For me the Cornish landscape means a lot. I've been to other places where it's been lush and soft but I haven't felt altogether happy in it. The openness of the landscape appeals to me, this sense of being on top, exposed, and yet, in a way, it makes you vulnerable, but in the present state of international art, environment and place seem to have less importance.

Another Cornish-born painter, Margo Maeckleberghe, of Penzance, when asked why Cornwall attracts painters:

> I've thought about this a lot. This crystal-clear light, I think is the explanation. It gives everything a new meaning, form and structure of the landscape is defined and enlarged by it. The atmosphere is so very stimulating, savage, strong, primitive, beautiful ... it's all these and much more besides. Words are really inadequate. The most important part, to me, is this mysterious x, an artist must *feel* about a place to paint it and be true to his art. Light, atmosphere, shimmering of pale, bleached grasses, surging half seen rocks, mist, rain, storm and sun on moors and headlands and, of course, skies, skies and skies ... this is part of what I try to paint. The coasts, seas moors, skies and rocks of Cornwall offer inexhaustible painting material ... the peculiar clarity of light which throws this landscape of West Penwith into sharp perspective. It's a land of great antiquity,

primeval and sometimes savage. Why, the skies, even on a hot day, hold threats of storm clouds and the clouds, by their shadows, give form to the landscape below ... and the light shining through can give exciting effects. Turner, the greatest British painter, I think, spent most of his life painting the effects of wind, rain and storm. There are, of course, many ways a painting can begin. It can be an idea which ties up suddenly with something seen, more often it's a logical development of a previous painting. It's not the beginning, it's often the end or the middle, when the difficulties are greatest.

I draw and sketch a lot ... literally hundreds. It might be a movement of a wave over submerged rocks or a thrusting granite headland. Drawing lays bare the bones of the landscape for me, it's like a map into a strange country, it helps to build an image, but it can never be the complete image. One constantly rejects, selects, searches again ... an interesting stone from the beach, a lichen twig, a piece of seaweed ... they can all help to start the chain reaction for the beginning of a painting ...

Margo Maeckleberghe is one of the most exciting painters now working in Cornwall precisely because her work reflects the strange intangible way in which Cornwall, the land, the place, does in fact influence, indeed enter into the artist. In her landscapes the Cornish imagery is so vital and striking that it almost seems to come alive before your eyes – a line of thought enhanced by her most recent series of Atlanta paintings, in which slices of Cornish landscape and coastline merge mysteriously into the shape of a reclining woman.

Interestingly, another woman painter, Misome Peile of St Ives, underlined a similar point when she once confessed that she gave up drawing for three years to learn to think and feel only the painted surface. Hundreds of action-drawings of the wilderness of Carbis Bay, close to her studio, enabled her to break through to the fusion of sky, land and water under the brilliant hillside light – now she sees the human form 'in all landscape and in the heavens'.

And on the subject of the Cornish landscape, this is what Dick Gilbert, also Cornish-born, has to say:

It works on me. Take just this one valley where I live. If I stayed here a hundred years I shouldn't have exhausted its painting possibilities. You get this feeling of place. The Cornish landscape exhibits a constantly changing occurrence, it has a large visual depth or distance, in other words you can see a lot of land relative to the sky, whereas in other countries the land is frequently at a distance, but the visual depth is small ... in Cornwall there's more land in the visual experience.

With Dick Gilbert one is turning to the field of abstract art. It is not without significance that so many abstract artists have been drawn to Cornwall (and rather amusing that because the landscape is so impressive not even the abstract artists have been able to keep it out of their work). I recall some interesting remarks on this point by the late Charles Marriott, one-time art critic of *The Times*, in suggesting that West Cornwall was in particular a draughtsman's country. He felt strongly that seen from a height such as Trencrom or Carn Galve the landscape ran to a decorative pattern, a sort of cloisonné effect of little green fields inset in a network of gorse-clad hedges, and he had the notion that even in their abstractions, painters such as Ben Nicholson got nearer to the peculiar magic of West Cornwall than did the painters of earlier years.

Ben Nicholson, who came to live in Cornwall in 1939 and spent the next twenty years in his adopted county, once expounded further on the abstract artist's outlook. He saw painting and religious experience as the same thing, a search for the understanding and realisation of infinity – an idea which is complete with no beginning, no end, and therefore giving to all things for all time. The structure of Cornwall, he confessed, suited him ideally:

I want to be so free that I even would not need to use free colour. I dislike the idea that a picture is something precious, the painter something special. There is an artist in everybody. That was the reason why I welcomed the technique of collage. One discovers new things. One does not paint only in one medium, it does away with the precious quality of easel in picture. Art is work and play for me. And work and play are as necessary for me as breathing.

Yesterday I began to paint the garden gate. As soon as my hand touches a brush, my imagination begins to work. When I finished I went to my studio and made a picture. Can you imagine the excitement which a line gives you when you draw it across a surface? It is like walking through the country from St Ives to Zennor ...

Another abstract painter, John Wells of Newlyn, had this to say:

So all around the morning air and the sea's blue light with points of diamond and the gorse incandescent beyond the trees; countless rocks, ragged or round and of every colour; birds resting or flying and the sense of a multitude of creatures living out their minute lives. All this is part of one's life and I was desperately eager to express it; not just what I see, but what I feel about it and beyond it ... but how can one paint the warmth of the sun, the sound of the sea, the journey of a beetle across a rock, or thoughts of one's own whence and whither? That is one argument for abstraction. One absorbs all these feelings and ideas; if one is lucky they undergo an alchemistic transformation into gold and *that* is the creative work.

It is hardly surprising that sculptors, in particular, have been most profoundly influenced – one might even say uplifted – by Cornwall. This is especially so today; but there was one Cornish sculptor, Nevill Northey Burnard, who made his mark in the early nineteenth century and whose work was marvellously commemorated in a poem by Charles Causley, painting a vivid picture of the sculptor working away at the moorstone until at last he 'quietly lifted out his prize of rock'.

Every sculptor who comes to Cornwall is confronted with this exciting chance of lifting out his 'prize of rock' – more so, surely than in any other part of Britain. For, and it cannot be too strongly emphasised, Cornwall is essentially a land of granite, a land whose agelessness is somehow symbolised by that very stone.

Barbara Hepworth, once married to Ben Nicholson, became the most famous sculptor to be associated with Cornwall, and her tantalising and inimitable and often beautiful pieces of polished stone now adorn galleries all over the world. For the last thirty years of her life Barbara Hepworth lived and worked at her Trewyn studio (now arranged as a memorial museum open to the public) and though her work might be termed abstract it is literally possible to see and feel the Cornish influence in shape and form.

To anyone who studies Barbara Hepworth's work it is obvious that in Cornwall she found her correct setting. From her garden she could look out across St Ives and its bay to distant hills; and all around her was the Cornish scene, in all its mystery, with an impact so continual that it was bound to infiltrate into her own carvings. A London critic, Michael Williams, in reviewing an earlier exhibition of her work at the Lefevre Gallery suggested that she had come under the influence of Cornwall because 'that landscape, perhaps more than any other, must call up a deep emotional response from one so much of whose life is concerned with digging deep into the heart of her materials and searching out basic forms.'

While Ben Nicholson directed the attention of younger artists to the abstract qualities implied in the Cornish landscape, Barbara Hepworth opened a similar pathway into an understanding of the qualities of a sculptor's materials, especially seen against the background of a world peculiarly dominated by ancient stones. Rosewood, alabaster, mahogany, Portland stone and blue limestone were all used by Miss Hepworth to produce her now familiar shapes and forms. She appeared obsessed with the beauty and significance of natural formations of these stones and woods; but at the same time she had a profound ability to capture the lineaments of the human form, and at many of her exhibitions visitors were surprised at the imposing array of drawings in oil and pencil of the human figure.

There was, for instance, a most fascinating series of drawings of figures present at a hospital operation. Even in her drawings, however, one was always conscious that they were mainly roughouts for eventual interpretation in wood or stone. There is something remote and impersonal – indeed purely abstract – about Hepworth figures which suits very much the mood of our scientifically obsessed civilization. In Cornwall her art flowered, perhaps more fully than it might have done anywhere else in Britain.

Sven Berlin was another sculptor who always declared that it was Cornwall which helped to release and develop his ability to create living things in stone, the stone being an entity in itself with a centre of vitality and tension that could be made to exist in space. I once asked Sven Berlin to put into words some of his thoughts about his reaction to the Cornwall around him and feel he captured something important in these words:

The open coliseum of each little cove of sand or rock may be the theatre for any natural, supernatural or unnatural agent. The unending presence of the sea breathing ceaselessly over the shoulder of each hill, the rock charged with a thousand sunsets or carved by a hundred years of rain, the little trees loaded with berries growing away from the prevailing wind, offering crimson to green, the mind's incessant vertigo at the cliff edge, and the slow constructional flight of the seagull – these things in some way act as the charming of magicians and open up the deeper rooms of experience in man, making him aware of his being part of the natural universe, at the head of a great unseen procession of gods and devils, spectres and dragons, of being a channel for unknown and undefined forces; of facing the mystery of life, awakening powers of perception which search beyond the frontiers of normal events.

That extract was used in Berlin's book about Alfred Wallis, the old St Ives fisherman turned primitive painter who, at the age of seventy, began painting in housepaints on old pieces of cardboards, a flood of child-like efforts which today are on the walls of numerous art galleries and treasured in many private collections. At first sight many of Wallis's paintings do, indeed, seem like the sort of pictures pinned up on classroom walls in infant schools – but on closer inspection one begins to have second thoughts, particularly in his last terrifying Death Ship paintings. The fact is that this gnarled, turned-in, suspicious, pernickety old Cornishman was impelled to give creative expression to what was there, in his own land, in similar way to intuitive outsiders like Berlin.

Wallis was not the only primitive painter of Cornwall. Jack Pender's grandfather, W.J. George, another fisherman, also started painting in his old age, producing hundreds of canvases from the age of seventy-five until his death at ninety-four. One of these was described by his grandson like this:

> Three black boats, brown mizzen sails steadying, white foam creaming their bows, hurrying to Newlyn fish market. Past the granite and white cottage homes of their crews, past the reaching arms of their home harbour, past the protecting island that forms a natural breakwater to the one time busy fishing village of Mousehole. The urgency of their progress is witnessed, felt, recorded.

'Witnessed, felt, recorded' – that is what every painter of any stature who works in Cornwall seems somehow to be compelled to follow. It can be seen in the primitive work of a Wallis or a George, or Mary Jewells of Newlyn, or Bryan Pearce of St Ives – a courageous figure suffering from phynylktenuea, a rare disease that retards mental progress, who nevertheless has produced armfuls of fascinating studies of Cornish towns and landscapes seen through his extraordinary perceptive eye.

In the works of the simple primitive artist the same thing is reflected, although more starkly and directly, that is to be found in the less simple work of abstract painters like Ben Nicholson or John Wells, or in the sculpture of Sven Berlin – or Barbara Hepworth, who, as most art critics agree, was deeply under the influence of Cornwall.

Go into any art gallery in Cornwall – whether the more sophisticated galleries of the Penwith Society at St Ives or the Newlyn Society at Newlyn, or the smaller galleries to be found in Polperro, Looe, Boscastle, Padstow, Newquay, Fowey, Falmouth – and certain interesting factors will emerge.

First, by far the greatest percentage of the painters exhibiting will be non-Cornish – artists who have been drawn to Cornwall and have settled here to work. Second, the variety of their work, and that of their Cornish companions, is quite remarkable, ranging from traditional to pop, from figurative to abstract, from landscapes to geometrical formations. Thirdly, and this is the really significant factor, with the possible exception of portraiture, it is almost certain that every single painting or sculpture will somehow reflect that Cornish environment out of which it has been created.

That environment is difficult to pin down directly. Of course, from a superficial point of view there are many obvious aspects of very definite importance in their own way. For instance from the sheerly economical view painters' studios are not to be found growing on trees – in most parts of Britain they would be an unusual feature indeed, but in Cornwall they are in fact, plentiful. St Ives is perhaps something of a special case, but it is worth noting that in this small fishing town alone there are probably upwards of fifty professional artist's studios, all occupied by working artists; some of them, like Porthmeor and the former Piazze Studios set overlooking one of the most beautiful beaches in Britain.

Similarly in Newlyn, in Mousehole, Penzance and surrounding areas, artists' studios are to be found in comparative profusion, often tailor-built; but equally often converted successfully from former barns, even cowsheds. Where there's a will, there has to be a way. The same can be said for many other areas: Polperro, Fowey, Looe, Falmouth, Truro, Tintagel, Boscastle, Wadebridge. Indeed today the artist's studio in Cornwall is almost as commonplace as, say, a pottery in Stoke (though even so Cornwall can boast more potteries than any other English county).

X

Surfing Sagas

One of the pleasures forever associated with Cornwall in my mind has been surfing, a sport ideally suited to our wild Atlantic-washed seas. As a writer it has always been one of my aims to try and capture the elusive qualities of surfing. This has proved much more difficult than might be imagined but finally I like to think I achieved my aim by telling the story of my friend Mr Pemberton who came upon surfing as we often come upon the great revelations of life in an accidental sort of way.

Previously he had been almost a model of sober propriety, a solid, well-set up young man with aspirations to be something in the city. Along with a few million others he had caught his regular morning train from the suburbs, spent his quota of somewhat dull hours totting up figures, and sometimes dividing them again, and in general dutifully followed the somewhat uneventful career which his parents, if perhaps not nature, had mapped out for him.

It wasn't very exciting, let's be honest. It was hardly, shall we say, an exhilarating sort of prospect. All the same probably Mr Pemberton would have continued cutting for himself one of those familiar, and indeed quite comfortable ruts – if there had not been somewhere deep inside him, one of those tiny voices, those little rebellious streaks which, fortunately, haunt a good many human beings. The sort of niggling pinprick which sometimes made young Mr Pemberton stop in his tracks to stare wistfully at some sea-bound tanker puffing off to unknown horizons – or caused him to emerge from some enthralling adventure film fiercely twirling his rolled up umbrella preparatory to taking on a gang of bandits.

At least, one must assume it was something like this which brought surfing to Mr Pemberton – or to be more accurate, gave Mr Pemberton to surfing.

It happened one holiday-time when Mr Pemberton, for want of any more specific plan, had accompanied a party of men friends on a car tour of Cornwall. Like most visitors to this western tip of our islands Mr Pemberton was suitably impressed by the majestic moorlands and the rugged cliffs: but that might have been the end of matters, had it not been for that quite casual visit, one sunny but blustery afternoon, to a certain holiday resort along the North Cornwall coast. It was there, strolling along the wide sandy front, that Mr Pemberton chanced to look curiously seawards and perceive in their full fury and splendour, those legendary Atlantic rollers, pounding and sweeping over the glistening golden sands. Surely Nature could hardly provide a more splendid spectacle?

But – what was this? From out of the white-fanged jaws of this nautical monster there spat one – two – three – more, six – seven, perhaps a dozen – puny human beings. One moment, it seemed, they did not exist: the next, like birds on wing, they zoomed forward on the very crest of the huge waves and were shot at extraordinary speed along the surface of sea-washed sand.

Mr Pemberton had never seen anything quite so remarkable in all his life. To say that he was fascinated would be inadequate. He was mesmerised, hypnotised; he stood where he was, as if chained to the spot. In vain did his friends attempt to persuade him to continue with their stroll: their words were not only disregarded, they were not even heard. 'I'll see you later on,' muttered Mr Pemberton vaguely. But in some way, already, he was casting off anchor.

After a while Mr Pemberton climbed over the parapet and walked across the soft sands to be able to watch more closely the activities of the scattered group of surfers. He watched in open-mouthed admiration as these gladiators, arming themselves with not more than the flimsiest length of curved board, strode forth to do battle with the mighty sea. Even before they entered the water they looked puny and pitiful, and once they were surrounded by clouds of froth and surf, their minute helplessness seemed emphasised. Yet it was these same small heroes who, moments later, came hurtling on the sea's back with all the natural pride of true victors.

Mr Pemberton was not only amazed, not only intrigued – he was captivated. He walked up and down at the edge of the sea almost wanting to cheer the surfers on. Jolly well done, sir, he thought, as one very daring swimmer shot down a veritable mountain of a wave. Oh, good show, good show – as another figure executed an almost perfect landing at high speed. Oh – well done, well done, well done …!

It was then that the aforesaid tiny voice began to whisper in Mr Pemberton's ear those fatal words: *why not have a go yourself?* Why … not … yes, why not … indeed? The more Mr Pemberton listened to the little voice (it was louder now) the more the idea called to him, like some clarion rallying call. After all – he watched a man old enough to be his father float effortlessly upon the bosom of an enormous wave – there was no real reason why he shouldn't. He was on holiday, wasn't he? And he had got a costume, it was back in the car, there. Well, hurry then, snapped the insidious voice, as if just a little tired of having to whip up enthusiasm for a patently good cause.

Mr Pemberton hurried, he even ran most of the way back to the car. When he got there he found, to his consternation, that his friends were preparing to leave. This was perhaps a preliminary moment of truth: he did not waste time trying to persuade them to stay, he hastily removed his suitcase and murmured reassuringly that he would be all right, but he'd stay on here for a while, and see them back in town. Then, to the accompaniment of their concerted, astonished stare, Mr Pemberton turned and hurried back to those waves which, instinct told him already, would not wait for ever.

At the end of the parapet Mr Pemberton found a small hut where surf boards were offered at £2 an hour. Seizing the first that came to hand he plunged on down over the sands, seeking a suitable spot wherein to divest himself of encumbering clothes, and prepare for his great initiation.

Like all true-blue Englishmen Mr Pemberton clung to the belief that he could undress without exposing any important part of his body, a superhuman task involving matador-like manoeuvres with a small towel. However, at last the feat was accomplished, and Mr Pemberton – all white six feet of him – set course for the sea, clutching to his breast the long tapering surf-board.

It is perhaps some indication of Mr Pemberton's determined character that he was prepared to embark on surfing without any more experience than having watched, in some awe, those more professionally skilled than he. True, as he waded purposefully out into the shallow waters he kept a weather eye open on surfers around him: he noted that they tucked the base of the board into the pit of their stomachs, and that their outstretched hands held the top curve of the board at either side ... But then spectators at cricket matches can watch how Test batsmen execute their graceful and glorious strokes ...

When Mr Pemberton was in about three feet of water he turned, as he had seen the other surfers do, and waited. He was not, to tell the truth, quite sure what he was waiting for; but on the reasonable assumption that it was the next wave he glanced quickly at the approaching white wall, and obeying a blind wild impulse, most mistakenly, launched himself forward as he had seen so many other surfers do.

It must be admitted that the next few turbulent moments had a disturbing effect on Mr Pemberton's initial morale. Far from soaring forward gracefully, he was brutally knocked sideways, his surf-board was torn from his grasp, and before landing spread-eagled on the wet sands he turned two or possibly more somersaults. A lesser mortal might have retired there and then, but after getting back his wind Mr Pemberton gritted his teeth, retrieved his surf-board which was floating rapidly away, and plunged back into the fray, or rather surf.

Surf, Mr Pemberton now discovered, was a term synonymous of many things: a cloud of innocent spray, or a vast mountain of solid water – a froth of gentle rain or a thunderous downpour of Atlantic venom – it was all, technically, surf. The only trouble was that Mr Pemberton seemed unable to ride it. Indeed the simile was not inapt, for the sea seemed to have turned into a bucking broncho determined to unseat Mr Pemberton at every forlorn attempt to sit in the saddle. No matter how he tucked his surf-board in, no matter how fierce his grip, how pronounced his waiting crouch – whether he threw himself before or after or during a wave – none of it seemed to make any difference. The result, was depressingly the same, a cascade of drenching water, a forlorn tug of war with the surf-board, several loud splashes and gurgles and screams from Mr Pemberton – and the final ignominious delivery of his bruised and battered body on the bare sands.

How long this suffering might have been endured, who knows? – Mr Pemberton was doggedly determined to master his new craft no matter at what cost. But suddenly as he waded mournfully out again to meet yet another onslaught, it seemed as if some bright-eyed mermaid, some green-eyed wonder of the deep was sent to his aid. 'You are a silly boy,' she said in honeyed tones, 'You're doing it all wrong. Now look, just you watch me. Here's a wave coming, now one – two – three – go!'

As the wave boomed and broke all around him Mr Pemberton struggled to keep his feet, and looking around to see nothing but flying surf, decided the mermaid must indeed be a creature of his imagination. But no – as the spray cleared, he could just dimly see the dark crown of her head as she reached, triumphantly, the distant shore.

A few minutes later she was back at his side, whispering encouragement. 'Go on with you now, I was just as bad when I started. You just need confidence. Now why don't you come with me this time? Here we go then – watch out – one – two – three – and *go!*'

This time – this time, too, Mr Pemberton went. He went with the mermaid, with his surf-board – above all with the wave. It was as if he was caught up magically and marvellously, at least for a moment, by something altogether outside his previous . experience. It was terrifying, of course, quite terrifying; at one moment Mr Pemberton seemed to be poised high in space, like a bird – at the next, whoosh – and he was soaring, ah, yes at last soaring, down and down and down – terrifying, yes, but oh how wonderful, how marvellous, how exhilarating!

Words failed Mr Pemberton, as slowly he returned to this earth, while his surf-board planed gently to a stop at the tip of the wave-ridden beach. For a while he could only mutter and grunt, half with shock, half with pleasure.

'Hey, there,' called out that same honeyed voice. 'Once isn't good enough – you've got to do it again and again and again … '

Turning with a sheepish smile, and gathering himself once more for the fray (though this time more confidently) Mr Pemberton saw, it seemed to him for the first time, that his mermaid was a fairly realistic image of a brown and healthy, and rather pretty young girl in a bikini. Her name, it later transpired, was Pam.

But none of this really mattered at the moment. All that mattered was to get back into the water, to wade through those first shallow waves, to venture further and further until the mountains rose around you, and then at last – like the matador with his bull – to seek the moment of truth, that instinctive time of knowing – *Now*! and to launch yourself, like an eagle into flight, upon the incoming wave.

It would be untrue to say that Mr Pemberton spent every remaining moment of his holiday surfing. There was a need to eat and sleep, and also to improve upon this miraculous meeting with a mermaid called Pam who turned out, conveniently, also to come from London. And yet surfing was the peak, the ultimate – in surfing Mr Pemberton suddenly understood himself, was released, consumed, and returned to himself a gayer, more exhilarated, more exciting person than before. There were moments, as he caught a particularly high wave and came riding in at a speed which if not greater than light he felt sure was ahead of sound, when he knew he was with the gods themselves. Somehow he knew, and if he didn't that little voice, rather bolder now, would have told him, that after all this, a dull life in the city would never be enough … which in the event proved exactly so, although fortunately by then he had the added permanent advantage of a mermaid's company.

So perhaps next time you go surfing you had better be very careful ... and then again, perhaps not.

Unfortunately upon reflection I could not help feeling that my tale of Mr Pemberton only covered one aspect of surfing – that is, from the amateur's point of view. During the days we lived on the edge of the great surfing beach of Porthmeor we became acutely conscious of the very professional element, young almost full time professional surfers ... somehow I felt I ought to try and capture their more professional attitude. Finally (I hope!) I did this about a group of professional surfers, telling how every summer day they drove far out along a sandy peninsula, then went down the sloping dunes, carrying their brightly coloured malibu boards over their heads. There were three of them: blonde, bronzed, lithe, looking curiously alike so that they might have been brothers. Everything about them was planned and purposeful: they moved across the long flat sands steadily, in unison, and somehow, as they approached the distant white-crested waves, they seemed almost to merge into a single, magical entity. From that scene sprang a short story:

'...The young girl with the pigtail and the innocent eyes watched them avidly from the moment their rakish green car appeared over the brow of the hill until their distant, glistening brown figures plunged into the sea ... and, of course, that was only the beginning of her watching. For then, once in the sea, the three surfers seemed to become something more than merely human: they were princes of light, young gods, indeed, strutting daringly in the face of danger. At first they squatted patiently on their boards, waiting, waiting ... and then, when at last one of the big, rolling waves mounted up, so they jumped up upon their slender boards, poised to soar away on their marvellous, magical journeys.

'That was a sight, indeed, the three of them skimming effortlessly along, the sun painting their taut brown bodies a golden sheen, and the snarling, frustrated sea frothing angrily about their feet. In such a manner the young girl sometimes watched them surf along for nearly a quarter of a mile before at long last their boards touched the sandy bottom and they leaped clear to avoid being turned over ... A few moments later they would gather up their boards and be marching back into the thundering water, eager to swim out in readiness for the next big wave.

'And once again the young girl would be waiting and watching: all afternoon, for as long as the young gods chose to stride across their salty domain, so she would lie in her vantage point among the dunes, suitably secretive, yet with a grandstand view. And what sights she witnessed! Why, sometimes it seemed as if a mountainous wave would rear so high that it must surely swallow up the puny, tantalising figures; her heart would be in her dry mouth, fearfully; yet somehow they always managed to preserve their balance, weaving cleverly from one crest to another, occasionally playing tricks on the angry waves by leaning this way and that, at last cutting triumphantly down the cascading face of a wave. Oh, there was no end to the spell-binding daring of it all, to the beautiful intricacies, the secret skills. Mesmerised, tongue in cheek, eyes rounded, imagination on fire, the young girl could have watched, forever and ever, her shining young gods.

'And when at last they picked up their boards and marched back across the dunes and finally drove away along the bumpy lane, the young girl throbbed so much with the memories that she could hardly wait to run back home across the fields to the long, low bungalow where she lived with her widowed mother.

'"Mother, mother!" she would cry out, hurrying into the kitchen, "Oh, you should have seen them today!"

'And whatever her mother might be doing, she would have to stop and listen to the streaming imagination of the bright-eyed young girl, remembering the day's magic.

'At first the mother only half listened to her daughter's ramblings. But then one day a word or two stuck in her memory, so that she began to pay more attention. Although she had plenty to do all day, or, to put it more accurately, she filled up her time with housework, she could not deny that hers was now a very lonely life. The bungalow stood far from other houses, and there were often times, despite her daughter, when she felt a very solitary person. She could not help remembering the life of the past with her young husband; a man about the house, in the evenings, and in the bed.

'"Well, then," she said, one day. "These surfers – do you think maybe they would like a cup of tea after they've finished?"

'For the young girl the suggestion at first bordered on the ludicrous. A cup of tea ... for the golden gods! It didn't seem right; it was an impertinence. But then the thought of what might be achieved, the miracle of seeing the gods in her own home, before her very eyes – this gave her courage.

'So one day, when the surfers were trudging back across the beach, she came out from her hiding place and scampered across.

'"My mother says – would you like a cup of tea?"

'She was too shy to stay for their reply, and scampered away again hiding her scarlet face. But she turned just before going into the garden gate, and saw, to her dread and elation, that the three surfers were following across the dunes.

'"They're coming!" she cried out to her mother. "They're coming!"

'When the three young men finally knocked at the front door the girl remained lurking in the background, while her mother went and answered. She heard everyone mouthing the usual polite remarks, and then, almost before she knew what was happening, they were all standing around in the sitting room – looking, in their brief swimming trunks, just a little incongruous.

'Their names were Mac and Doug and Sandy, the young girl learned. She was too shy to ask herself, but her mother soon extracted the information, putting them all at ease with a surprising skill. Somehow the young girl had always thought of her mother as old, but now she realised this was not so. She began to study her mother's physical appearance, noting that she still had the trim figure of a much younger woman. And in addition, she was – well, curiously alive. Or so it seemed that afternoon as she stood chatting to the young surfers. Shy, no, indeed, the young girl had never before noticed her mother so alive, her eyes bright, her cheeks flushed, her voice singing away.

'And the surfers, they were alive, too, but in a different way. Their aliveness was written into their movements, the texture and colour of their brown skins, the ripple of muscles, the swift turn of a blonde head ... The young girl was relieved to find that nothing had been lost by the transition from the shimmering landscape of the golden sands to the confining walls of the sitting room. Indeed, in some ways, the impact was more forceful ... it was impossible to be in that room without being almost painfully aware of the glistening presence of three young gods, perhaps from another world.

'When at last they had gone the young girl waved to them excitedly from the garden gate: and then returned to the house aglow with a sense of proprietorship.

'"Well," she said animatedly, coming into the living room. "Well, what do you think?"

'She had been going to say a lot of other things, but somehow the sight of her mother cut off the words. Her mother looked so unfamiliar standing there all aglow and alive: almost like a stranger.

'"Well –?" began the young girl again, rather uneasily.

'"Yes, my dear," said her mother, softly, smiling faintly. "They were very nice. Very nice indeed."

'She paused, and then went on lightly: 'Shall you bring them to tea tomorrow?'

'After that the surfers began to call in most afternoons. They were always very polite about their approach, knocking dutifully at the front door and waiting before entering ... but alas, as they became more at ease, so they began to relax and behave more naturally. This was noticeable in their attitude to the young girl's mother. At first they were respectful, almost filial: then, as the ice was broken, they began to unbend. Mac, the eldest of the three, who was good-looking in a military way, with a neat toothbrush moustache and wavy blonde hair, was the most charming and attentive, in a sophisticated manner.

Doug, his close companion, was more the strong, silent type, who seemed to express everything he had to say merely by his bovine presence. Even Sandy, the youngest and thinnest of them all, only a lad really, hovered around the mother enthusiastically.

'Watching, the young girl became intrigued. She had never before seen her mother so vivacious, so much the centre of things. She had even taken to dressing up for the occasions, would spend half an hour before the surfers were due to arrive, trying on this dress and that one – sitting in front of the mirror, examining herself critically; sometimes, grudgingly, asking for her daughter's opinion.

' "Do you think this suits me? Really?"

'And again:

'"Green – I wonder if green is right for me? Someone once said it matched the colour of my eyes."

'The young girl had not before wondered if her mother's eyes were green or not; nor even, really, how her mother might appear in other people's opinions. But now she became aware of her mother in the purely physical sense: how she stood, how she moved about, how she wore her clothes – how, indeed, she sparkled.

'"You're really awfully pretty, mother."

Her mother swung round, flushed.

'"Am I? Do you really think so?"

'The surfers thought that, too: the young girl could tell this from the way they clustered around, sometimes quite avariciously, as if vying with one another to be the closest. Why, sometimes she could hardly see the fluttering figure of her mother for the encircling wall of sun-tanned human flesh. Mac, leaning forward confidentially, Doug standing solid and attentive; even Sandy cocking his close-cropped head anxiously, youthful body curved forward, eager not to miss anything.

'One day Mac told an amusing story that made them all burst into laughter ... and as he did so, quite casually, he put an arm around the mother's shoulder. It seemed a natural enough gesture, yet it worried the young girl. She began to study the man called Mac intently, as if seeking to understand what he represented. And when one day, as she was watching, puzzled, her mother, with a wholly unfamiliar gesture, put up a hand and quickly pushed back a lock of Mac's blonde hair.

'"That's better,' she said brightly. 'You look better with your hair brushed back."'

'And as if to emphasise some point, she ran her hand roughly through Mac's hair, ruffling it as one might a dog's.

'But then, just as the young girl was attempting to assimilate this happening, so it seemed that, even despite herself, her mother had turned so that her gaze fell upon Doug, standing as usual in his strong silent pose at her side ... Doug, who was bigger and stronger and more handsome than any of the others. And it was a strange thing, but the young girl had a marked impression that, although her mother only looked quickly at Doug, somehow that look encompassed everything. It was almost as if, in a way, she had touched him or there had been a secret embrace.

'The young girl looked away, embarrassed. And before the surfers left that day she went out on her own, wandering among the sand-dunes. From there she watched the eventual departure ... but now, somehow, the three god-like figures did not shimmer quite so brightly, their images were strangely tarnished.

'When finally the girl went home, she found her mother sitting by the window, smiling to herself: looking once again almost alien.

'"Hullo, dear," said her mother: and the girl was silent, waiting, almost instinctively, for what was to come.

'"By the way, that Mac," went on her mother, casually. "He's nice, isn't he? He's taking me out tonight ... you won't mind, will you dear? We shan't be late back."

'When Mac brought her mother home later that night, the young girl had gone to bed. But she heard the sound of their return, the movements in the living room, the tinkle of cups as her mother made a cup of tea – a great one for cups of tea was her mother. After that she heard nothing more, and eventually she fell into a troubled sleep.

'The next day her mother made no reference to the previous evening: and somehow, to the girl's surprise, the surfers came round as usual for their cups of tea. Outwardly there appeared to be no change in their general behaviour: her mother was very friendly to Mac, but then she made herself pleasant to the others as well.

'All the same, she went out again soon afterwards with Mac: and again, and again.

'"Yes, he's a nice boy, Mac," said her mother: and that was her only comment.

'And yet all the time the young girl could not help noticing that her mother often had her eyes fixed not on Mac, but on Doug. Doug, the strong and silent one; Doug, the handsome, primitive one – Doug, who kept to himself, glowering, yet visibly restless.

'Soon the young girl's feminine curiosity grew so strong that she could not resist asking.

'"Doug – what about Doug? I've seen you looking at him sometimes."

'"Nonsense!" declared her mother. "Whatever makes you think that?"

'"But I have, really I have," said the young girl, looking at her mother intently.

'"You must be mistaken. Why should I look at Doug?" said her mother, appearing to shrug. But the young girl was quick to notice the way, even at the mention of his name, her mother's expression changed ... and how she opened her mouth and poked out the tip of her tongue, thoughtfully.

'"Doug ... What a funny girl you are."

'Soon after that Doug came round one evening, unexpectedly. At least, the young girl presumed it was an unexpected call. He stood awkwardly in the doorway while she went and fetched her mother and then continued to look ill at ease, even sitting in the living room. The young girl kept wondering why Doug had come round, and looking at him curiously, so that he became quite uncomfortable. After a while her mother said, quite sharply: "Isn't it your bedtime, dear?"

'So she went to bed and lay there, unable to sleep, trying not to think about what might be happening in the nearby living room (near, and yet so far): above all, trying not to remember the last sight she had, her mother standing by the mantelpiece, one white arm outstretched, looking quite excited ... and Doug, standing almost at the other end of the room, as if frightened to be any nearer, his eyes dark and heavy-lidded.

'It seemed incredible that despite all these diversions the afternoons continued as before: the green car driving up, the brown figures walking across, the white waves closing around their ritual visitors ... and then, later, the familiar ring at the front door bell. Sometimes the young girl felt that this must be the way life had always been; the scene unchanging, her mother dispensing cups of tea, the lithe brown bodies arched round, herself watching from a distance, in the background the eternal boom of the sea.

'But then in her heart she feared it was not the same. She could not put her finger on the point of change, could hardly define her feelings; but she remained aware of a growing dissatisfaction with what was happening.

'One afternoon, as the usual routine appeared to be following its pre-ordained course, the young girl started to her feet, overwhelmed by a suffocating feeling of being hemmed in by the walls, the brown bodies, the clatter of tea-cups ... She felt she must get away and be alone: hastily she went out of the rear of the bungalow and ran across the fields to the long white sands. As she ran she closed her eyes sometimes, as if to hold back strange tears that threatened to spurt out ... "I wish, oh, I wish ..." she cried out, to the wind, to the vast empty sky, to the waiting sea.

'When she reached the water's edge she began walking along, head bent low, as if searching for some explanation to the mysteries of life. She walked on and on and on ... and only when, tired, she paused to stare about her, did she become aware she was not alone. Standing quite near to her was the third of the surfers, the young lad called Sandy.

'"Hullo," he said awkwardly.

'"Hullo," said the girl.

'He made a vague gesture.

"'I saw you run out."

'He said no more, and the girl made no attempt to reply, and for quite a while they stood as if in a trance ... until at last the oncoming waves began to lap around their feet.

"'Hey." said Sandy, with a smile. "Mind, or you'll get your feet wet."

"'Oh, I don't mind," said the girl, a little breathlessly. "I like the feeling of the sea."

"'Do you?" He looked at her with sudden interest, and she saw that his eyes, which had always seemed a little weak, were suddenly crystal clear and a hard, bright blue, as if the mere mention of the sea brought him vividly to life.

"'I love the sea," said Sandy, emphatically.

"'Yes, that's what I mean," cried out the girl, afraid she had not made her point. "I *love* it, too ... and watching you all surfing ... it's marvellous."

"'Yes," he agreed, gravely. "It is marvellous."

'There was a pause, and then he looked at her almost timidly.

"'Have you ever done any surfing?"

'The young girl grimaced.

"'No, of course not. I don't know how to; why, I'd never be able ... "

'She became aware of him looking at her in blank amazement.

"'Of course you would. Of course you would."

She shook her head, but he would have none of it. Indeed, all at once he became startlingly, pleasurably dominant. He insisted that she went back and changed into her swimming things at once, and then he would take her out surfing. She would soon learn, he said airily.

'The young girl ran all the way back to the bungalow and crept round to her room at the back. In the living room the others and her mother were still chattering away. Quickly she slipped off her clothes and donned her black swimsuit, and then she crept out again and went scampering across the sands. As she did so she looked up and saw the slight figure waiting for her at the water's edge, leaning on the malibu board. For a moment the image was so precise and personal that she halted, a little afraid. Then, looking again, it seemed to her that she could not see merely one, but many – many brown-skinned young gods, waiting to enfold her into their magical kingdom. Suddenly, she grew excited, aware as if by instinct that she was already older and wiser, and therefore equipped for new worlds, greater marvels.

'She began running on, faster and faster, her hair flying in the wind, her breath coming in spurts, her eyes brighter than ever before.

'"Coming." she cried out. "I'm coming … "'

XI

When the World Was Young

Listening idly to the radio one afternoon I came across one of those always popular programmes where someone, usually a celebrity of some sort, remembers something of past importance – perhaps the most significant day in their lives, or for instance, 'the most unforgettable character I ever met.' Inevitably this set my mind racing back into our own past, and certainly I had no difficulty about reconstructing my own special memory of a truly unforgettable character.

In fact I heard of Miss Jenkins long before I ever met her. It was during a time in my youth when every summer we went to spend our holidays at Llanfairfechan on the coast of North Wales. We used to stay with my Aunty Lil in a quiet house off a cobbled terrace near the beach. At the end of the terrace, much higher up, there was a huge white gate labelled: PRIVATE: NO ADMITTANCE. Behind that gate, in a huge granite house that was all corners and gables and dropping ivy, lived old Miss Jenkins. Alone.

I suppose it was this quality of aloneness that always caught my imagination about Miss Jenkins. At first, as I say, I learned of it by hearsay. We would be sitting out in our porch late of an evening and perhaps a single light would flash out high up in the old gabled house. My Aunty Lil would shiver slightly and pull her shawl round her shoulders, and then, as if reminded of something, she would pat me on the shoulder.

'Now, then, come along, time for your lovely hot chocolate.'

But as we turned and went in, invariably she would glance over her shoulders at that lonely light and I can always remember the meaning way she would murmur to herself, 'Tut-tut, the poor soul...'

I was about thirteen at the time, that curious half-way stage between childhood and teenage wisdom: an introspective time, when one's imagination grabs hungrily at half hints of worlds and ideas beyond immediate comprehension.

'Why is she a poor soul, Aunty Lil?' I said.

But of course I had no satisfactory answer, was merely shushed off with my hot chocolate. That night I lay in bed and thought about Miss Jenkins, all alone in her big house with the forbidding gate. Why did she live there all alone? How did she spend her time? Why did she behave in such odd ways?

As time went on I became more familiar by personal experience with Miss Jenkins' oddities. Her manner of dress, for instance, was often peculiar. Sometimes I would catch a glimpse of her pottering about in her overgrown garden, wearing a dressing gown of bright yellow and black stripes and a large white panama hat ... while her feet, I noticed, were bare. On another occasion I saw her mowing the lawn with great ferocity clad in a voluminous garment which my aunt later told me was a pre-First World War bathing dress.

But perhaps Miss Jenkins' greatest oddity was her habit of appearing on a noisy auto-cycle, clad in a black leather coat and gaiters, and a fearful conglomeration of goggles and leather helmet. It was not often she emerged in this way (it seemed to me about the only occasion she ever left the seclusion of her own house) but there was naturally great competition among the local children to witness the event. At the sound of the angry phut phut of Miss Jenkins' rickety machine they would stop playing games and even leave meals and dash out to lean over the garden walls and stare, open-mouthed, at the fearsome apparition. And of course, as the bike and Miss Jenkins disappeared down the road they would break into shrieks of laughter.

But somehow I never felt like laughing. I suppose Miss Jenkins' loneliness must have touched a chord deep in me, without my knowing. I could not help thinking about the person behind the mask of goggles. What was she really like?

Then one day, quite accidentally, I found out. Not in the familiar environment of the village, but way up the moorland road, up by the side of Penmaen mountain with its rambling boulder-strewn flanks spotted with green and yellow clumps of gorse. I had wandered up there one hot and sunny afternoon and was about to turn off the road when I caught a glimpse of a familiar leather-coated figure bent over a prostrate auto-cycle.

Going nearer I found Miss Jenkins tinkering with a spanner at the engine. 'Er – can I help you?' I said awkwardly.

Filled with the children's lurid tales I half expected her to turn round in a fury – or perhaps to scuttle away, like a witch disturbed. I was surprised when, instead, she looked up quite placidly.

'Aren't you the little boy at the cottage down the road?'

'Yes,' I said. As I spoke I was secretly staring into Miss Jenkins' face, maybe half expecting to find reflected in it some ogre-like sort of characteristics – but seeing, instead, what must once have been a rather lovely face, now lined with time and worry, yet still bearing a certain nobility and delicacy, and enhanced by two strong, almost jet black eyes that peered at me fiercely.

'I don't suppose you know anything about auto-cycles that won't go?'

'No,' I had to admit.

'That makes two of us. Well ...'

It seemed that with the unexpected advent of company Miss Jenkins was glad of an excuse to forget about her troublesome bike. Indeed, she turned her back on it completely and strode to the edge of the road, looking over the panorama of fields and distant sandy shores.

'It's lovely, isn't it?' I ventured. And then, after a pause. 'Have you ever been to the Giant's Chair? You get a better view there?'

Miss Jenkins sniffed and seemed about to say something, but in my eagerness I interrupted.

'Yes, really. It's over there – come with me and I'll show you.'

Looking back I can only suppose that my childish impudence captivated Miss Jenkins, so that almost meekly she followed in my wake. If anyone had seen the curious procession, a young boy leading a large goggled leather coated figure up a lonely track, they would have assumed it was another of Miss Jenkins' eccentricities. But in fact it was I who took Miss Jenkins to the Giant's Chair, she who obediently followed and finally sat by me on the wide slab of granite which someone, giant or otherwise, had set up in such a magnificent position.

As if pleased by my fulfilment of my promise Miss Jenkins looked about her quite jubilantly and, misled, I began pointing out spots.

'That's Beaumaris over there ... and see, there's the old mine shaft, and over there you can just see the tip of the lighthouse, and the bay – look, the sea's quite rough...'

'Child, child,' said Miss Jenkins, not unkindly, 'I was born and bred here – I know all these places like the back of my hand.'

'But you didn't know the Giant's Chair?'

A curious smile softened the parchment face.

'Well, it *is* a long time since I came up here, I must admit ... a long time. Maybe I had forgotten ... a little.'

I didn't know to what she was referring, but obviously it must have been something terribly important, for the recollection seemed suddenly to loosen Miss Jenkins' tongue. Now she began talking about those distant past days, not altogether, I felt, directly to me, yet needing me as an audience. I have often tried to remember more exactly the things she talked about, but somehow their detail is lost in a haze. But I do remember the strong feeling underneath, the curious sense of tender regret, almost of painful memory, of something precious that had been lost. I had some sort of picture of a young Miss Jenkins with long black hair and beautiful white skin and a slender gracious figure, the world at her feet, the horizon fully of rosy promise ... and of someone she had loved, romantically, tenderly, who had perhaps loved her, too ... and then of something happening, something going wrong... and suddenly there was Miss Jenkins, old and tired, withdrawn into her shell, living alone and shut away in her secret unhappiness.

I suppose I must have felt this almost in a physical way, for I remember putting out a hand and taking Miss Jenkins' gnarled fingers and pressing them gently. And then I said, regretfully, I had better be getting home or my parents would be worried.

So we went back to the road and Miss Jenkins picked up her bike and began wheeling it back alongside me. We must have looked an odd couple, and yet somehow we were in harmony. When, just before she left me, Miss Jenkins asked me to call in for tea the next afternoon, I was delighted.

All the same I didn't say anything to my parents about the visit, nor the others that were to follow. From the beginning I sensed, or perhaps I decided, that my experience with Miss Jenkins was something quite private, and perhaps, I now think, unique.

She wasn't at all the cross, wizened old witch one might have supposed from the local tittle-tattle. She was a tall, wiry old lady with a wry and humorous nature, full of secret laughter, and gifted with an imagination that seemed to bubble with all kinds of bizarre ideas. I suppose I was the spark that set her off, I with my thirteen innocent years reaching out to her across all the decades. She must have been nearly seventy, yet in a way in my company she became young again, perhaps the young Miss Jenkins who had once stood on the threshold of all sorts of wonderful and glorious things. I even thought sometimes, looking at her shyly as she sat by her sitting room window looking out at her favourite marigolds, that she looked young and pretty again.

Perhaps I was imagining things? It is difficult to say. We used to meet, rather like conspirators, two or three times a week, and once together the outside world seemed to recede and become unreal. *This* was the real world, this strange old house, most of whose rooms were dusty and empty, this house given up to Miss Jenkins and her memories. Photographs, trinkets, heirlooms, pictures – they were all constant reminders of experiences I could never know.

And which, bless her heart, Miss Jenkins never wanted me to know. That was the only time I ever knew her to be cross, the time when once I began to say, excitedly, 'Oh, when I grow up I do hope I live in a big house on my own like you and – and –'

That was the time Miss Jenkins face went almost dark with

anger and she stamped her foot several times, and her black eyes glowered.

'Child, you must never, *never* talk like that again. Because when you grow up – ' and her voice softened suddenly. 'When you grow up, my dear, I want you to fall in love, to marry, to know what it is to have a *real* home, children of your own, a whole fulfilled life … '

She paused before the picture she had painted, and then said, almost in a whisper, 'Yes, I want that for you so very much, my dear.' And perhaps only many years later was I old enough to really hear and comprehend the undertones of yearning for what might have been, beyond that wish for my own fulfilment.

I suppose that summer came to an official end, as all summers do, and I went home with my parents. The funny thing is, in some ways I often think it never ended. Some years later Miss Jenkins died, and her big old granite house was taken over by a family from up country and turned into the inevitable guest house … yet somehow it didn't seem to matter. I like to think that even now, though I have been married for over thirty years and there are grandchildren's voices echoing around the walls of our home, yet in a strange way Miss Jenkins shares a part of the joy it has all brought me. because, you see, in that distant summer I learned from Miss Jenkins, who never found it, that there is nothing so precious in the whole wide world as love.

Yes, Miss Jenkins has always remained a vivid memory of those days in Wales. So, too have 'The Girls'. There were four of them: Dilys and Megan and Llys and Kate.

We were children then, all of us, full of life and laughter and gay innocence, happy in our carefree holiday existence. The girls lived at the old vicarage, with its long, rather battered walls, its decayed drive and rusting iron gates. They were Thomas Lloyd's daughters – at least, Dilys and Megan and Llys were, and Kate was an adopted daughter. Not that you would have known any difference, for Mrs Lloyd mothered them with the same sweetness, and if anything she seemed to have a special care for Kate – in those days very much the babe of the party, with her round eyes and her small, serious face, and her golden hair curled up in ringlets.

I can even remember as far back as the time when the others used to come along wheeling Kate in an enormous dilapidated pram into which, besides Kate, they would stuff dolls, macintoshes, sailing boats, oranges, apples, loaves of bread, books, several packets of sticky sweets and two or three table trays. I would be waiting at the cross-roads with some of the other local boys and then the whole straggling procession would meander up the winding mountain road that led to Bryn Mawr and nearly all our adventures.

That's what the trays were for, of course. Bryn Mawr was a gentle, friendly sort of mountain – you would sit yourself on one of those smooth trays at the top and toboggan down the tight grassy slopes – down and down and down until you ended in a plateau of soft green grass. Mind you, it wasn't all that easy. All over the sides of the mountain there were great clumps of yellow-flowered gorse bushes, and if you landed in one of those you'd be sore for weeks. The art of tobagganing of course, was *not* to land in a gorse bush. We were all quite proficient but none of us ever attained the ease and skill of the Girls. I think myself they used to creep up on dark nights and practise in secret. There was something so complete, so confident about their performances that we did not mind giving them best, squatting down on the grass and watching them, one by one, as they swooped down the mountain-side in graceful succession.

Dilys went first. Dilys always went first: not only because she was the oldest, but because she was the wisest – yes, and the gentlest and the kindest and the best of a lot of other things. We all loved Dilys, rather as one loved a mother. She mothered us all, sisters and friends and foes alike. It was impossible to dislike her, impossible not to acknowledge her qualities. She was a big-boned, strong girl, the strength in her features as well as her body. She had black curly hair cut short, so that she always had a faintly boyish look about her. But there was nothing boyish about her behaviour, and something immensely maternal about the way she would sometimes pick up little Kate and carry her in her arms, rocking her gently in imitation of a real mother.

Megan and Llys would be second – together. It would have been more than anyone's life was worth to have differentiated between them. In age Megan had the advantage of a bare year, but all their lives they had fought for the privilege of being second to Dilys. I remember at picnics on the beach – races, fought to the last inch in which Megan and Llys wouldn't give in. I remember, later, when we were of an age to go dancing, the scheming and counter-scheming that went on between those two. They were both so attractive that was the trouble. And in such different ways, too. that made it even harder to choose between the two. Megan's was entirely a physical attraction. She had deep black eyes and a full curved mouth that could mock anyone to the point of distraction. When she laughed her teeth shone and her skin gleamed and her eyes danced with light – she glowed and burned with some fire of her own. I could never take my eyes off Megan – not for many years.

Llys was quieter. Megan was the torrent in full stream, Llys was the tiny mountain stream trickling onwards. Both reached their destination. Llys was a dreamer, and a dream. She was Welsh, like Megan and Dilys, but she was the oldest, most eternal Celt – that dark image of mystery which seems to brood invisibly over the slopes of Cader Idris, the misty heights of Snowdon, the sudden peace of Idwal. She was a slim, untidy girl, with wild dark hair that was blown about by the slightest breeze, so that she was always pushing it back.

I shall never forget going down to Llantyllan beach late one August evening and coming upon Llys standing right out at one end of the wooden pier. She wore an old pair of canvas trousers and a voluminous red corduroy three-quarter coat. I was hardly conscious of her figure: there was just Llys, her face turned upwards towards the dying sun over Anglesey, her long black hair fluttering out into the breeze, her eyes closed as if she was looking into some secret place which nobody else could see. She seemed, that evening, like a symbol – not only of Wales, but of other things – of all those elusive things which men chase into a receding distance, never knowing if they are real ... and in the end, not wanting to know, for fear the illusion might shatter like a broken mirror.

The Girls ... From the top of Bryn Mawr you can see across to Anglesey, to the grey houses of Beaumaris, to the little detached hump of Puffin Island. We used to hire Ivor Hopkin's boat sometimes, perhaps a dozen of us, and row across to the island. There was a small shingle beach where you could pull the boat up, and then go sun-bathing among the rocks and the puffins and seals.

Once I went across with Megan. We crept away, like two conspirators, and took the boat without Ivor knowing. It required more effort than usual to get across, and all the time we were secretly wondering what would happen if the wind changed and a rough sea blew up so that we couldn't get back. When we landed we pretended we were shipwrecked. Megan pouted her mouth and teased me, and we chased each other up and down the length of the island.

Megan was as strong and agile as any man, and it was half an hour before I finally caught her, pinned against the corner of a rock. I held both her shoulders with my hands, tight, and tighter: and then suddenly I pulled her towards me and kissed her. I had never kissed anyone like that before. She kissed me back with her wild and generous passion, that was as stirring as it was misleading. Later I made a ring out of grass and wound it round her finger. Some day I vowed, it would be a real ring. And Megan's eyes danced at me and laughed, and laughed; but she said nothing, and in the end there was nothing I could do but take her in my arms again. It was late when we got back, and there was a row about the boat. Somehow I expected everything to be different after that, but it wasn't. Megan wore my grass ring for a few days and then it just disappeared. She never wore it again, though I often kissed her, and always with that same desperate, almost angry passion.

A year later, when I was working in London on my first job as a cub reporter, Llys turned up. She had come to do her training as a nurse. She was living in a hostel, but she had a fair amount of spare time, and it was natural she should contact me. How strange it was, seeing London for the first time through Llys's eyes. She, the dreamer, made London a dream. We did all those things that the tourists are told to do. We got up early one morning and went to Covent Garden to watch the fruit and vegetable lorries unloading. We took a riverboat from Chelsea to Gravesend, sniffing the curious river odours, building up fantasies about each of the semi-derelict tugs and boats that were moored around on the mud banks while the tide was out. Now and then we came upon a large steamer with its name written boldly in white or yellow paint, in strange foreign lettering.

'Fancy,' Llys whispered, leaning over the rails and staring with all the intensity of her deep, dark eyes. 'Fancy, that boat has been all round the world – perhaps even further?'

That was Llys's approach to life, to each incident. Everything was a potential wonder. Even going on a Sunday evening to the Welsh chapel in the heart of the West End – even that became a mystic experience with Llys. We crept into the back row and became part of the congealment of exiles. We sang ourselves out of our alien surroundings, back into the dreamy world of faraway Llanfairfechan.

Youthful memories – I have one other that comes to mind, a case of first love, indeed. There was this boat left high and dry up the estuary, lying on its side at a point on the inside bend where incoming tides regularly deposited their flotsam. Each tide crept up round the keel and even lapped the tilted under-deck, but the waves lacked the strength to drag the boat back. And so the living sea rose and fell each day, but the boat lay there inanimate, a dead and abandoned thing, long and sleek, with the outline of an old lifeboat but the built-up decks of a sloop, cabin and all.

The boat that had appeared mysteriously from nowhere, belonging it seemed to no one, for there had never been any inquiry about her in twelve months or more. The boat whose white and green paint had faded, whose brass was rusted, whose mainsail was in rags, whose port-holes were jammed up. The boat which in some curious, indefinable way for us

children still held in its slender heart some remembered beat of
unknown, exciting life.

It was Karen and I who found the boat. Some of the other
kids used to come along with us afterwards, of course, but I
think perhaps they recognized what we felt to be true – that the
boat was ours, Karen's and mine.

I can remember the day we found it, remember it more
vividly than all the other events of half a century since. Perhaps
that will be my last thought of all – the memory of Karen and
myself playing among the sandhills. Karen crying, 'Catch me if
you can' and disappearing shrieking over the top – and I,
following, stopping as she had done, mouth agape, staring
down to where the sea had left its offering.

'A boat!' Karen cried out in her eager, high-pitched voice,
with a lilt of its Celtic fatherland. 'Quick, let's go aboard.'

We had hardly set foot on the heavy sodden planks when we
looked at each other excitedly, exhilarated. This surely, must
be ours – our boat. So when the other children came later, I
suppose we must have expressed this attitude quite naturally.
And how proudly we showed them our discovery!

'Look, there's a real cabin. There are two bunks inside, still
with blankets, though they're a bit wet, of course.'

And Karen bubbling with excitement – 'Like to hold the
wheel? Look, you can turn it this way and that – just like a real
sailor.'

Soon we were all sitting in the cabin, like conspirators,
laughing and giggling.

'Fancy,' one kid whistled. 'The tide's coming in. Supposing
we float away?'

But Karen and I shook our heads derisively. We knew, you
see. We had spent most of a day on our boat, and we knew she
was embedded pretty firmly. We believed fervently she was
here for ever – for us.

After that we used to come down a lot to the boat. Karen's
parents and mine were great friends. We had been growing up
together ever since I could remember. She was thirteen, then,
Karen, and I was a year older. A strange midway age when you
feel too grown up to play like the wild children of yesterday,

yet too young to be able to enter fully into grown-up activities. An age when Karen had her hair still plaited in long pigtails, yet once appearing wearing a pair of nylon stockings. An age when after I began to wear long grey flannel trousers, I blushed scarlet before everyone's teasing.

The only one who didn't laugh and tease was Karen. 'I think you look nice', she said, and we went off, bound together even by that tenuous sympathy. So you see our interest in the boat wasn't merely childish. It was more than that – oh, much more. It became for us, well, a sort of refuge, I suppose. A refuge from our parents when they were cross with us, or wouldn't take an interest in our affairs. A refuge when things went wrong at school. A refuge, even, from each other. Once I remember, we had quarrelled, and Karen disappeared.

It was an hour later until I thought to go across the field between the humped sand dunes and down to the beach. And there was Karen, lying on the deck of the boat, sunbathing. When she saw me she turned her head away without saying anything; but I guessed she was pleased I had come. I climbed up beside her, and we lay in contented silence, dreaming our dreams in the bright afternoon sunlight.

That was how the boat crept into our intimate lives. I used to think if we came down one day and found it gone, the sands barren and empty of that familiar shape, it would have been like the end of the world. Sometimes, indeed, we worried about this happening. Often in the evenings, after supper – as the tide crept up the estuary, with a relentless inevitability – we would meet up by the golf course and stroll down and across the sandy dunes to the sea. We might pretend we were just taking a casual walk, but our destination was always the same.

When we reached the boat we would climb aboard and sit with our legs dangling over the side of the deck, watching uneasily the progress of the oncoming tide. Sometimes, as the frothy waves whirled round the bottom of the boat, we would become alarmed and look at each other in momentary panic. And though our past experience told us the tide always turned before the boat was properly afloat, we could not suppress our fears.

Then, perhaps instinctively, we used to go down the narrow stairs into the cabin, and sit on one of the narrow bunks, holding hands in sudden communion as we willed the sea to go away, to leave our boat alone. I can remember the last time that happened. We sat there and heard the bubbling of the waves round the hull. And then at last the sound, like the waves themselves, began to recede, and we knew our boat was safe once more.

There was an almost full moon hanging high above the bay, flooding the estuary with silvery light – the boat and us, as well. I looked at Karen and she looked at me, and it was a moment of rare magic. We felt the planks of the boat firm under our feet, the slight breeze ruffling our hair, and we could easily imagine we were sailing away into the darkness, embarked on some glorious adventure.

Such a peaceful and silver and magic time was that evening. Karen and I and our boat, dreaming in a sleeping estuary.

And yet, only one evening later, the world was gone. The silver moon had vanished, the sky was a mass of evil dark clouds. The wind was howling and the sea – the sea boiling up like something possessed by a demon. We had never seen anything quite like this before. We had listened indulgently as old fishermen talked with awe of some particularly bad storm of the past – as if hearing a tale from a story book. But this was reality; wind howling in telephone wires, whistling among the reeds on the sand-dunes – and in the distance, the sea booming and thudding like nemesis.

Karen and I came out of our homes at the same time. I can remember holding her by the hand and running – but it was different from other times. Now everything was dark and fearsome and full of threats.

'Oh, Denys, suppose – suppose –'

When we got to the beach we found the gale blowing straight down the river mouth, whipping the waves up into great walls of white froth, driving them on viciously up the sandy slopes on either side. Already waves were breaking upon the side of the boat. Karen gave a quick cry and ran forward.

'Come on, hurry!'

I suppose we acted without thinking. We splashed through water and climbed on to the boat. Her decks were wet with spray and her mast and stays creaked before the wind.

'Denys!' Karen said in anguish, standing there, her hair blowing wild, and spray on her face. 'What shall we do?'

And even as she spoke, she seemed to move by instinct towards the hatch of the cabin, as if in some way believing that the old habit could still avert danger. Suddenly I began to feel frightened; maybe some sort of sixth sense. I stood on the deck, acutely alert. A wave broke over the side, splashing me. At the same moment I felt something I had never felt before – a movement of the boat itself, a shuddering, unwilling fearful movement.

Then even as I wondered uncertainly if I could possibly take a rope and pull the boat farther up the shore, a second wave broke over again drenching me. This time the boat wavered from one side to the other – and there ahead I saw more waves booming up the estuary.

I came to life and cried out, 'Karen, Karen – where are you?'

The boat began rocking backwards and forwards. I felt the motion in my feet; it was like beginning to fall on a slippery slope. I rushed to the top of the cabin stairs and jumped down two at a time. She was sitting huddled in the farthest corner.

'Karen – the boat's moving.'

For a moment she did not move. I can remember how my heart went out to her as I guessed what she was thinking – our boat, our secret proud possession, helplessly rocking in the arms of a gale. And then instinct, fear, too, perhaps, took hold of me and I stumbled across the tiny cabin.

'It's no good – you've got to come.'

My hands felt for her, touched her slim shoulders, pulled her insistently up and towards the hatch. I half guided, half carried her up on to the deck. Outside there was a touch of fantasy about the scene. The boat had reared more steeply, water foamed and cascaded about. Suddenly we were afloat and being tugged by the waves into the seething centre of the raging estuary waters.

'Jump, Karen!'

I gripped Karen tight, tighter than I had ever held her before, and together we jumped into the water. As we did so there was a roaring, sucking noise behind us and the great bulk of the boat seemed to swirl round and spin away from us.

We landed up to our waists in water, soft sand under our feet. I held Karen steady with one hand and used the other like an oar to help fight our way towards the bank. When we were free of the water we stopped and turned. Somewhere out in the centre, occasionally silhouetted against the phosphorescence of the white crested waves, our boat was visible. We watched it caught up in the maelstrom, tossed this way and that, but gradually receding as the tide went on the turn.

'Oh, Denys!' Karen's voice echoed strangely out of the darkness. 'She'll be washed away.'

And worse, I thought grimly. She would be smashed up into pathetic pieces of wreckage to be washed up on distant shores. But suddenly – standing there, feeling the ultimate protectiveness of my arms round Karen's shoulders, knowing she nestled close as if she would never leave me again – suddenly I felt a curious calm. I knew the boat had become a symbol, a sacrifice perhaps; and that as its white and green skeleton was finally swallowed by the angry waves – out of its loss might come unexpected gain. Suddenly on that wild, dark night, I knew I would never be alone again. I knew Karen was with me, wet and warm and living, more magical than any dream-boat. And I knew, as we watched the storm racing away into oblivion, we would always remember that on the night we lost our boat, we found something even more wonderful and precious.

But I mustn't ramble on too much … in the end, like so many other girls, Karen and 'the Girls' vanished into their separate worlds and I was left to embark on my own life. Obviously my years on the coast of North Wales made as deep an impression on me as my subsequent years in Cornwall, and I suppose for a Celt this is hardly surprising. I often think there are many similarities between the two lands, though when it comes to defining them the task suddenly becomes difficult. The people for instance are not very alike – the Welsh are a happier and more outward going race, whereas the Cornish always seem rather dour and turned in.

Superficially, too, the lands, can seem different – certainly as to scale, for in Wales everything is rather huge – mountains and lakes and quarries and so forth. In Cornwall the highest hilltop, Brown Willy, is puny put beside Snowdon. The coastlines too are very different, that of Wales is much flatter and more sandy. And yet it is in the landscapes and seascapes that finally the similarities are to be found – not, as I say, superficially, but where they find a common link – atmosphere. Standing on the side of a lonely Welsh mountain one can be aware of the same sort of brooding sense of the past as comes over one standing upon some Cornish cliff. In other words the past is impregnated into Wales as it is into Cornwall, in a physical way, so that it is impossible to escape.

Looking back I recognise how lucky I have been to experience twice in my life this almost mystic sort of relationship with a specific place. Now, after more than thirty years it is Cornwall that looms largest in my consciousness! All the same, if only because it is forever associated with my long lost youth, Wales will always have a secret place in my heart.

XII

The Haunted Land

The other night the BBC broadcast a whole programme from the Scilly Isles with interviews with people living on Tresco and the other offshore isles. Listening I was reminded at once of what a strange place the Scillies are – how different to other parts of Britain. They have an atmosphere, a strange brooding presence ... But then, too, so does this end of the land corner of Cornwall. The fact is that we who live in West Cornwall, whether the Scillies or Penwith, do in fact inhabit a haunted land. You would have to be blind and deaf not to react to this atmosphere. Appropriately enough it was the now blind and deaf Cornish poet Jack Clemo who, looking back over many years to a time when he could see, could still visualise:

> Clay land dawns and sunsets, the first golden rays of the sun striking the white peaks, setting the metal prongs and tipwires glowing and shimmering while the gravel bulk remained in shadow, and then at evening the daylight fading mysteriously from the blurred grey masses and the weird spiked cluster of stacks ... at night a fairyland touch with the June lights, pit lights and tank lights twinkling, and the red glare of a furnace occasionally glimpsed through a kiln doorway.

This view of a man-created interior part of Cornwall is just as weird and haunting as the effects of nature. Cornwall is mainly fashioned by nature and here there are some wise words contained in Ithell Colquhoun's *Living Stones*.*

* Peter Owen 1957.

160

The life of a region depends ultimately on its geological substratum, for this sets up a chain reaction which passes, determining their character, in turn through its steam and wells, its vegetation and the animal life which feeds on this, and finally through the type of human being attracted to live there. In a profound sense also the structure of its rocks gives rise to the psychic life of the land; granite, serpentine, slate, sandstone, limestone, chalk and the rest have each their special personality dependant upon the age in which they were laid down, each being co-existent with a special phase of the earth spirit's manifestation.

West Penwith is made up of granite, one of the world's oldest rocks, a substance instinctively associated with endurance and inflexibility – interestingly enough the basic elements of the Cornish character – and as Ithell Colquhoun suggests, the fundamental fact about Cornwall is that if for some reason you do not like granite, then you will literally never be happy there. If, however, like most people, you experience an instinctive response to a granite boulder hung with grey and golden lichen, especially if set high on some lonely moor or above a raging sea far below, then you are likely to feel at home. And to feel at home in Cornwall, as I have tried to indicate is an experience which appears to have been shared in particular by artists and creative people of all kinds – something which in itself suggests that Cornwall is a very unusual environment in which to live indeed. You are always aware of its tremendous age and secondly, that, despite all the ravages of wild weather and the intrusions of human activities of various sorts, of its richness in pre-historic remains. Charles Woolf, Bard Don Delynyans of the Cornish Gorsedd, has suggested that for its size Land's End peninsula has the greater concentration of these than any other area in the county.

In particular the area is scattered with high granite masses that, though obviously belonging to a dim past, nevertheless have a look about them of having been constructed. Many people feel that such constructions, whether quoits or old crosses, are really 'holy rocks', emanating quite powerful radiation forces (or as some would prefer to say, psychic forces). This all fits in with the now popular theory advanced by John Michel in his book on the old stones of Cornwall, *Lost Atlantis*, in which he suggests that Cornwall plays an all-important part in the scheme of things as envisaged by the ancient creators of ley stones (which can be identified quite easily from the air), a series of ancient stones linking one with another, as far as the eye can see, across much of Britain. These ley stones symbolically reflected a mystical philosophy of life and appear absolutely normal in a place like Cornwall.

Of course it is important to recognise the right stones, the ancient ones, and not to be misled by more conventional erections; monuments and statues, such as the huge granite cross on top of Carn Brea to commemorate Sir Francis Bassett, of Knill's Steeple at St Ives which, in Ithell Colquhoun's words, have no inner vitality and exhale a mausoleum's chill.

How different in quality are the stones surrounding an ancient well! Either they have absorbed the virtue of the spring they guard or have themselves been 'hole rocks' before their incorporation within the shrine – often itself a perpetuation of the earliest lore though nominally converted. Old stone crosses, too, are full of psychic life; some are older than Christianity, examples of the masculine cross; others, like the Wendron God to whom hats were but lately still doffed, were sanctified menhirs before they were carved with the cross form. Some, indeed, are Christian, but had the Celtic Church not some praeternatural contact that later orthodoxies have lost or been denied?

Circles of stones play a large part in the mythology of my part of Cornwall. There are at least half a dozen such circles, one of which, Boscawen near St Just, is made up of nineteen stones – the same number as is associated with the south-east of Stonehenge. (Once every nineteen years the Sun God was due to appear to his worshippers when the approximation of lunar and solar lie occurred, and nineteen years was the length of the Sacred King's reign). Close to Tresidder, there is the famous stone circle known as the 'Merry Maidens', on the road from Lamorna. Legend has it that the stones represent the forever-frozen forms of maidens who dance on a holy day.

There are other strange stone edifices, too like Men an Tol, with a ring like stone through which one is supposed to crawl in the nude as a cure for rheumatism. There is a similar stone, the Tolven, near the Helford River; also an adjoining large stone called the Maen Pol. Apart from such ancient statues, the Penwith moors abound with cromlechs and carns, not forgetting the fascinating prehistoric villages, like Chysauster, just above New Mill, and Porthmeor, near Gurnard's Head.

It is impossible to wander among such settlements, or to pass thoughtfully around huge stones like the Lanyon Quoit, or for that matter to explore the fogous, that is, man-made caves of Rendeen, Boscastle, Lamorna, Hollangye and Carn Euny (the latter, under Government control, being open to the public), without being constantly reminded of that saying of George Meredith's about the past constantly being at the elbow of the Cornish.

You can never forget when you stand on granite, imponderable backbone of Cornwall, wheresoever you may wander, that it is *the land of the Celt.* For so many people Cornwall is still the home of the legendary King Arthur, often around the coastline, as at Mousehole, you will come upon a Merlin's Rock or at Sennen an immense stone called the Table Men supposed to have served the King as a dining table (while of course Dozmary Pool on Bodmin Moor has long been recognised as the abode of the Lady of the Lake). The spirit of King Arthur in fact permeates most of Cornwall: Castle D'Or, home of Iseult's husband, King Mark, is set up the River Fowey; Lamorna Cove has associations with the name of Sir Modred by whom Arthur met his death; and having once seen an electrifying performance of *Tristan and Iseult* at the Minack Theatre on the cliffs at Porthcurno, I am quite ready to believe that it was from some such romantic cliff that Iseult's ladies stared anxiously out to sea, watching for the all-important glimpse of the sail of the ship bringing news of Tristan's life or death (the black sail, falsely hauled up, caused Iseult to kill herself). And, of course, this is without even beginning to consider the region of Tintagel and Boscastle, rich in legends of Arthur and Guinevere and company, with the impressive ruined castle set on its headland amid ruins of a Celtic monastery, and Merlin's Cove cut into the cliffs below.

Wherever you wander in Cornwall, whether it be along the sea-racked shore or up among the inland moors, it requires very little imagination to summon up all kinds of haunting apparitions of the past, and of course there are numerous legends to fan the flame.

One of the commonest is of the fearful spirit of John Tregeagle who haunts Cornwall from coast to coast, pursued eternally by friends or by the Devil with a pack of headless hounds. One of the numerous herculean tasks he was set to earn penance for his sins was the perpetual emptying of the Dozmary Pool. Fleeing from that he sought refuge in the weird crag known as Roche Rock, a landmark for miles around, with a fifteenth century chapel of St Michael's, including a hermit's cell, perched on the summit. Built of granite the building literally seems to grow out of the rock. Tregeagle is supposed to have thrust his head through the tiny chapel window for sanctuary, but disliked equally the hermit's exhortations inside and the shrieks of thwarted demons without, so howled 'louder than all the winter tempests', so that none of the local people ever dared go near the place. Not, that is, until by some further spell poor old Tregeagle had been wafted away to a lonely beach in North Cornwall where he was set yet another endless and hopeless task – making ropes of sand at the edge of the sea!

Headless horsemen, Zennor mermaids, sunken cities, lost lands, village wenches turned into stone – they are all part of what the Cornish poet and novelist D.M. Thomas aptly calls 'the granite kingdom', a place whose scenery could indeed be said made to match its players. No wonder Cornwall has been described as sloping to hateful sunsets and the end of time. And yet – and yet, even then, even at Land's End, Cornwall has not ended. There is still that stretch of twenty-eight turbulent miles beyond which (and you can clearly see them on a clear day) lie those fascinating, fairy-like humps, the Isles of Scilly. Still more granite, still more legends, as in these lines extracted from a longer poem by Geoffrey Grigson:

Here are the islands of dead hope;
And where the bodies safely crouched,
The megaliths, empty on the headlines lie,
In the red, wind-shivering fern
High on these islands of a grim goodbye ...
And soon beyond the reddened fern, the rounded
Granite, gold on this green-black sea,
Day darkening with the night's destroying fear,
Must rise the flattened, huge and butter-
Yellow moon, which cannot care.

Cornwall has been described as oppressing all who come under its spell with that vague foreboding felt by a sleeper waking from sleep, haunted by the confused images of night – an untamed land, enduring sullenly the trappings of an age far from those remote twilights when with flint and stone man first sought to tame its wildness. Brooding over the happenings with which his fate has small concern, the heights look down on square fields where with much labour a victory has been won over the casts of moor and boulder-strewn upland – and even in those small plots of green the granite shoulders its way through the soil and many among them are relics of victories won in vain, little broken dwellings whose builders have gone and whose walls have crumbled back upon the earth ...

It is mainly in the wild and rugged coast-line, that one is most aware of the haunting and brooding atmosphere of the Cornish landscape, two inland areas like Bodmin Moor which can also create an immediate sense of unease. An interesting aspect of the inland areas is the way man-made intervention has somehow accentuated the same general feeling of weirdness, of other worldliness. For instance, according to A.C. Todd and Peter Laws in their *Industrial Archaelogy of Cornwall*, the face of about 45 square miles of the county around St Austell has over the past 200 years been transformed into a kind of lunar landscape, characterised by deep pits and quarries and huge grey and white pyramids of waste materials (just as the excavations go down to some 300 feet so do the mountains of waste rise up an equal distance).

This part of Cornwall, stretching from Fraddon and Melder in the west nine miles eastwards to St. Blazey, and from Roche in the north for five miles southwards to St Stephen, is china clay country. China clay, a stone containing special and peculiar properties of kaolin and feldspan was first discovered around 1745 by William Cookworthy at Tregonning Hill near Germoe, in West Cornwall. Later Cookworthy explored further east and finally found major sources of supply in the Austell area, where before long open-cast mining was begun by various small companies later forming the huge English China Clay Company (themselves now part of the International Rio Tinto Zinc Mining Group). In those early days the impact upon the county must have been quite an extraordinary one, as is indicated in this quotation from Mrs R.M. Barton's *History of the Cornish China Clay Industry*:[*]

> A scene then probably unique in the world. In all directions lay busy clay pits, round and oval ones; square pans filled with liquid clay; overhead launders (long wooden troughs for carrying liquid) attached to pumps forming a skeleton roof; the constant passage of bonneted and aproned women carrying clay blocks to reeders, drying sheds or drying grounds. Children, who earned 7d a day, collected moss to fill the joints between the granite blocks of the pans which allowed moisture to pass through. The creaking of pumps, of horse whims and the rushing of countless water engines ...

Today under pressure from environmental groups, the china clay industry is endeavouring to encourage natural growth to cover the ancient waste tips with grass, though the dozens of huge water filled pits remain so dramatically overhung by 'white mountains' which motorists suddenly see rising high against the skyline as they travel either east or west. Because

[*] Published by D.B. Barton, 1966.

china clay is in such world demand the industry is likely to prosper and expand for a considerable time: production is running at 20 million tons a year and the clay is exported all over the world for use in making rubber, plastics, paint, pharmaceuticals, inks, dyes, cosmetics and (the largest proportion) paper. Possibly now the biggest single industry in Cornwall, next to tourism, china clay even has its own special ports, at Par and Fowey, where the whole area often bears the unmistakable snowy taint of the clay dust, blown hither and thither by perverse winds. At these ports, notably at the docks up the River Fowey, large cargo vessels can be seen flying flags of Sweden, Denmark, Germany, Cyprus, Spain, Algeria, even Japan, and this, too, adds to the colourfulness of the landscape.

Where china clay, still a thriving industry, continues to make a strong physical impact upon Cornwall, one or two older industries, which now operate only on a comparatively small scale, have nevertheless left even more emphatic marks upon the countryside. I am referring in particular to tin and copper mining. In the words of A.C. Todd and Peter Laws:*

Those who may buy a cottage on a headland or in a valley winding down to the sea often hardly realise that from 1760 onwards Cornwall was as industrialised as the Midlands and the North of England. For almost 200 years it was one of the most important metal mining areas in the world, and became the setting for tremendous enterprises in the world of engineering, its blue skies shrouded by the smoke from a thousand chimney stacks, its wild life in fields, moors and lanes disturbed by the roar and clatter of machines. During the last century Cornwall yielded more than £200 million worth of tin and copper. Hundreds of shafts were sunk and thousands of miles of galleries driven with forest of timber erected for their support. Mountains of ore and rivers of water were brought to the surface and fleets of ships were required to bring coal to feed the boilers and smelters.

* *Industrial Archaeology of Cornwall*, David & Charles, 1972.

All this was soon to change: Cornwall, hub of the mining world, endured a tremendous slump and from a time when there were 300 water power mills, today, a hundred years later, there are now very few. The same startling collapse has taken place in the number of mines – where once there were hundreds, a few years ago the figure had dropped to two: at Geevor near St Just, and South Crofty, near Redruth – though with the revival of international demand for tin one or two mines are now being opened.

Disastrous though this regression may have been upon the Cornish economy, geographically it has left a very pronounced mark, as anyone who wanders about any of the old dejected mining areas will quickly observe. Just as the china clay white mountains create a bizarre extra dimension to that eeriness with which Cornwall is already associated by nature itself, so, too, the relics of those busy tin-mining days remain, like ghosts, to haunt the landscape. Sometimes it is possible to stand on some hillock, as at St Day, and look around and see rearing up against the skyline a cluster of a dozen or more of the old granite mining chimneys, warning fingers of fate from the past (the wooden parts of course having long since been looted for firewood). Local authorities have been careful to fill in or block off actual mine entrances, but here and there, there are still some remarkable monuments to this past era – notably at Botallack on the north west coast near St Just, where parts of old engine houses can still be seen rearing up against the sky and sea. (And Botallack, incidentally, with its tiers of exposed corridors, makes a fantastic sight from the sea). Then again there are the remains of the famous Levant Mine, scene of a great natural disaster in 1919 when parts of the mine shaft that extended under the sea collapsed with the loss of thirty-nine lives. To stand amid the chaos of Levant Mine in all its stark abandonment, say Todd and Laws, is to realise the shattering challenge facing an industrial archaeologist.

So perhaps it can be seen that the romance of these old and new industries, so much a part of the history of Cornwall, has contributed a very marked physical effect upon the Cornish landscape. I have a friend who lives up near the top of Ding-Dong hill, where the crumbling ruins still stand of a once active mine of that name. Here, high among the hills of Penwith, looking round upon great natural carns, gorse-covered moors, huge granite headlands, here and there strange edifices like the Lanyon Quoit, it is impossible not to include in this visual impression the weird shape of that old mine chimney rising up to the very heavens, stemming from a Cornish past that was most certainly man-made and yet now, somehow, has become part of the eternal mystery.

While considering the effect of local industries upon the actual shape and appearance and atmosphere of the Cornish landscape one should mention one or two smaller examples – slate quarrying, for instance. Physically this has not had such a pronounced effect as it has in North Wales, nevertheless in parts of Cornwall – most notably around Delabole in the north – quite large scale excavations have contributed decisively to the generally haunting atmosphere of the whole area around Tintagel and Boscastle. Here, briefly, is a portrait from an old handbook for travellers published in 1850 by the Royal Society of Cornwall:

Two villages owe their origin to the Delabole quarries, Pengelly and Medrose. These quarries present one of the most astonishing and animated scenes imaginable. The traveller suddenly beholds three enormous pits excavated by the uninterrupted labour of centuries, slowly encroaching upon the domain of the farmer. Throngs of men are engaged in various noisy employments, steam engines are lifting with a harsh sound their ponderous arms and raising loaded trucks from pit depths. Masses of slates slowly ascend on guide chains stretched like shrouds of a ship from the platform to pit bottom. The largest quarry is 260 feet deep. The slates, after blasting, are placed on a truck which is drawn up to the head by a steam engine, water being pumped from the quarry by a water wheel, and is then taken by waggon drawn by two bullocks and a horse to the beach at Port Gavorne to be loaded into ships.

Today the Delabole quarry is still functioning, and is now 500 feet deep and over a mile in circumference. There are various smaller quarries around, which make a striking impression on the unsuspecting traveller with their unusual blend of blue and brown and grey, rising on either side of the route from Camelford into Tintagel like surrealist hillocks.

There are granite quarries too in Cornwall: at Penryn, Mabe, Stithians, Constantine, Wendron, St Breward, Linkinborne, St Just etc. Waterloo Bridge was built with Penryn granite, and even the tiny quarry at Lamorna Cove, near Penzance, supplied large quantities of stone for the construction of the Thames Embankment. Most famous of the granite quarries is the De Lank at St Breward, near Wadebridge, a name known to stonemasons all over the world – and this business still operates. It provided the stone for the Eddystone and Beachy Head Lighthouses, as well as for the construction of docks at Singapore and Gibraltar. There are other quarried stones too, such as Polyhant, near Launceston, and serpentine, found in large quantities on the Lizard Peninsula. To this day the Lizard industry continues through individual craftsmen, working in a material that has been described as a beautiful marble of a dark green colour variegated with veins of purple, red, white and scarlet.

In the same way that quarries add to the atmosphere of a strange world, Cornwall's other two major industries, farming and fishing, contribute colour and atmosphere. Because Cornwall, jutting out so boldly into the heart of the surrounding seas, is so severely exposed to winds, the farming pattern has been to cover the land with small fields protected everywhere by the ubiquitous Cornish hedge (made invariably of loam and lumps of granite.) This is particularly so near the coast, where the land often acquires a tidy appearance that contrasts strangely with the often awesome and majestic lines of the cliffs and scenery. On some of the inland areas, particularly on huge open moors like Bodmin Moor, farming is of a different style, with few hedges, just vast areas of undulating arable land, lonely as the proverbial cloud save for here and there groups of grazing cattle of various sorts, including the famous Bodmin black ponies and, of course, sheep. Here again, the vast sweep of moorland and ever changing skies, often with racing, billowing clouds, make an unforgettable impression, what painter Lionel Misken envisaged as 'an almost brutally present structure suggesting petrified waves, crested at the tors, otherwise in deep wide undulations'.

The impact of the fishing industry also has a certain relevance to the landscape, for all round the Cornish coast there are picturesque little fishing ports with straggling cobbled streets leading up steep-sided hills lined with fishermen's cottages. I am thinking of such places as Mousehole and Newlyn and of Polruan and Polperro. From a distance one looks down upon a vista of toy-like fishing boats dotted about the waters of the harbour, of cottages which take on the appearance of doll's houses – a blended vision of Cornwall – as ever – as a place strangely apart and *different*. Sometimes, too, as at Feock and Rostranguet and Mylor, or at Fowey and Golant, on the south coast, or at Wadebridge on the River Camel on the North Coast, the fishermen element penetrates deeper into the countryside, flavouring some of the inland areas with the smell of the sea, the colourfulness of bright sails and painted boats, the tranquillity of fishermen in their blue dungarees sitting on cobbled walls watching the world go by.

Lest it may seem that all the mystery of Cornwall is contained in that far western tip (a view which you may well have sensed I incline towards) let me redress the balance by quoting briefly from some wise words of Michael Williams, who once wrote a book about riding on horseback across Bodmin Moor:

I have sat in the saddle on Brown Willy, grateful for a sturdy sure-footed cob, and watched the different worlds of Devon and Cornwall fade into a morning haze; a day when the wind slept and only birds and animals moved. I have wedged myself between rocks on Rough Tor and attempted to hide from the invisible knife of the wind – and both times I have been conscious of the same fact: Cornwall is a draughtsman's country. There is a sense of geometry in the landscape and even the sun, filtering through, intensifying the colours, cannot alter it.

It is indeed a draughtsman's country: a gaunt skeletal figure of stone, writhing and contorting into strange shapes, inhabiting a world of shadow and darkness where colour is neither particularly present nor really needed. In this bleakly defined form Cornwall may be said to achieve a curious kind of unity – the open and treeless surroundings of Tintagel in the east, for instance, being very similar to the bleakness of St Just, in Penwith in the west, and both surrounded by the same wide prospect of sea. Even on the south coast, though woodlands are to be found up one or two of the estuaries along the coast there is the same pattern of windswept treeless lands, the same awareness of a grim reality of life, whether by land or sea. Wherever you go in Cornwall – and indeed the *more* you travel and explore in Cornwall – I think you will come to recognise that here indeed is a granite kingdom that is very much its own domain. Perhaps more than that, you will be uneasily aware of a feeling put deftly into words by one of Cornwall's own poets, Charles Causley:

One day, friend and stranger,
The granite beast will rise
Rubbing the salt sea from his hundred eyes
Sleeping no longer.

In the running river he will observe the tree
Forging the slow signature of summer
And like Caliban he will stumble and clamour
Crying I am free! I am free! ...

Cast off your coloured stone ropes, signal the tourney!

And to the bells of many drowned chapels
Sail away, monster, leaving only ripples
Written in water to tell of your journey.*

An appropriate acknowledgement of the perpetual mystery!

*

And so I will leave this world of the granite beast and the haunted land and return, in conclusion, to my more immediate world of our beloved mill in the valley. At the opening of this book I told of the beginnings of yet another new saga, the efforts by our daughter and son in law to purchase Tresidder Mill, the next door property. Like all such sagas this had many ups and downs but in the end the deal went through and Alan and Gill suddenly found themselves in possession of – well let me quote from one of the original publicity blurbs:

Approached by a lane leading off the road from St Buryan via Crean to Polgigga, Tresidder Mill, set in a lovely and secluded valley about 2 miles from Land's End, is an interesting and unusual property comprising a main house, a converted mill and numerous other outbuildings, together with some $3\frac{1}{2}$ acres of land including sub tropical gardens, paddocks, fruit trees and woods. The main residence, all on one floor, consists of a lounge, 16 by 13 ft, a kitchen-breakfast room 13 by 8 ft, a dining room, $11\frac{3}{4}$ by 10 ft, a bedroom $11\frac{3}{4}$ by $10\frac{1}{2}$ ft, a second bedroom $8\frac{1}{2}$ by $7\frac{1}{2}$ ft, a third bedroom 8 by $7\frac{1}{2}$ ft and a bathroom and toilet. Cooking and water heating by oil fired stove, and there is main electricity, well water by electric pump, septic tank drainage and telephone. Nearby is a former mill comprising a large central room 16 by 12 ft, together with small dining-room. Among the outbuildings are a greenhouse, stables, stores, workshop, garage, etc. The paddocks are in fact large fields running down to the River Penberth. An outstanding

* *Collected Poems 1951-1975* (Macmillan, London Ltd).

feature is a trout stream and bridge just opposite the house front porch. Altogether the property offers immense possibilities either as a family home, or for holidays, or for riding, market gardening, etc. Although secluded, reached by a private lane, the property is close to several beautiful beaches—Porthcurno, Porthgwarra, Nanjizel and Sennen Cove – as well as the famous Minack Open Air Theatre. An excellent primary school is within easy walking distance and there are shops at Polgigga, Porthcurno and St Buryan (2 miles). The busy market town of Penzance is 8 miles distance – also within easy reach are Lamorna, Mousehole, Newlyn and St Ives. A property such as Tresidder Mill, in the heart of lovely West Cornwall, offers an unusual opportunity to anyone seeking a home in a beautiful and secluded setting

Once they had got over their initial shock at such a momentous event Alan and Gill soon went to work with a will at changing and improving their new possession – with help from time to time from the rest of the family. In the main the really hard work was done by Alan and Stephen. First they gutted the former old mill in the grounds and then adapted into its framework a small kitchen and bathroom – meantime Gill and Jess were busy clearing the sub-tropical gardens around. Day after day I could see columns of smoke swirling up as years of accumulated rubbish was disposed of – every fire, of course, being a source of great excitement to the five of our grandchildren (Paris, Armira, Amber, Cherry and Megan) who happened to be around (Ben and Lamorna were in London and newly born Morgan was over at St Just with Demelza). Next it was the turn of some of the various outbuildings, the stables being cleared out, two or three huts demolished, a pre-cast concrete garage actually physically moved to another spot altogether. Then there were drains to be checked, water supplies to connect – and of course half a roof to be repaired on the main house.

Finally – ending as I began – there was the little matter of the famous lane. Its potholes had become quite dangerous so at last we took action. Stephen hired a JCB and used that to level out the surface, then the next day we had two 10 ton lorry loads of gravel delivered, being dumped in a series of mounds along the winding lane. That was a busy day indeed for the whole family, and perhaps I might very well end with this very image, which came into my vision as I drove back from a visit to Penzance – there down the lane wielding rakes and shovels and brushes was a long line of members of the Val Baker family – Jess and Gill, Genevieve and Gina, Stephen and Alan – and of course, those delectable grandchildren – everyone working industriously and so speedily that long before nightfall the new surface was finished and in place.

As my car was poised at the top of the lane to me fell the honour of making the first journey down our as-good-as-new lane – oh what bliss not to feel the old familiar bumpity bump! – how peaceful and calm, by contrast, was my present journey.

Ah well, I thought, as I turned the car into the drive of our old mill, here's hoping all our other future journeys may be the same.